Over
Money
How to Bank on Your Dreams

Mind-over-Money
How to Bank on Your Dreams

Les B. Rich

CCC
Cash-Cut-Core

Published in the United States by Val Jayne Publishing

Val Jayne Publishing
PO Box 543
Highland MD 20777

www.cashcut.money
info@whatIwant.club

Printed in the United States

First Edition
10 9 8 7 6 5 4 3 2 1

ISBN 978-0-692-97844-3

Book Design by Valorie Jayne

ACKNOWLEDGEMENTS

Thanks to all the people, "family" and "friends" who tried to fling insurmountable obstacles in my path. They provided the incentive for me to overcome challenges, and develop my life in many surprising ways.

> "They tried to bury me, but didn't know that I'm a seed."
> *Mexican proverb.*

Many thanks to those who inspired me with their wisdom and encouragement. Thank you to my friend, Gertie Laury, who shows absolute support in all of my projects. Thanks to Barbara Mathis who helped with every aspect of this book. Special thanks to my friend Fred. You know who you are ... a shining star. Much gratitude to the masters of manifesting, too numerous to list. I thank you for helping to wake up the world to their true God-Given potential.

The poor man is poor because

he will not heed instruction.
Fred C. White

If you want to shine like the sun, you have to burn like the sun!

A.J. Abdul Kalam

Contents

YOUR MIND

Lacey Evans McDowell

Your mind is like a separate world
Where things are carried through.
Thoughts are people living there;
Dreams are things they do.
Emotions are the storms that rise;
Memory is the valley.
Cultured thoughts are works of art
Displayed in some art gallery.
Ambitions are the servants there—
Will-power is their master.
Carelessness, the enemy,
Can cause a great disaster!
Your thoughts, the people living there,
Are working just for you,—
And if you'll guide them safely,
They'll make your dreams come true.

1

Money Madness

A nickel ain't worth a dime anymore.
Yogi Berra

Money is our madness, our vast collective madness.
D.H. Lawrence

Money. Money. Money. I want Money—I need Money—I MUST HAVE MONEY!

"If only I had money. How different would my life be?"

Face it, money is the universal cry. There is no doubt that there is a very general impression that folks are mad for the Almighty Dollar. No use denying that the rush of the world is to be rich. It's apparent, however, that the majority of people do not reach a large measure of success in the fulfillment of their dreams.

For many people the problem of financial freedom is the most difficult to solve.

My trouble was that I believed that I was suffering from a "Money Famine." Literally hundreds of times we have heard this expression. It carries its own meaning. Just apply it to yourself. If you had the money to meet your obligations and buy what you want, there would be no depression for you. And what is true of you is true for all of us.

What about you? Do you want it? Do you need it? Do you have enough money?

Are you going forward today as you did yesterday, without a new plan, *thought* or hunch for the day? Are you satisfied with doing as you did last week, or last year? If you are, you'd better look out! For you're headed down that most intriguing, yet most dangerous of all highways—Route Rut—that broad, level stretch to Nowhere! On this thoroughfare, humanity is bumper-to-bumper, bunched up more densely than on any other. It's the easiest, quickest way to reach Rutland, Certainville and the City of Boredom.

Now you really don't want to go to any of these places; but it's so easy to arrive. And you know it! Habit. The habit of just doing what you are told to do, or no more than you are paid for doing, gets you there in a hurry!

But, down a piece leading off from Route Rut, there's a pleasant little bypath, that a few—just a few—choose to take in order that their happiness may be real and abiding. This bypass leads to New Lifeville, Joyland and Sunny Street—the places you've been seeking so long!

How do you get there?

Certainly not by taking home a bunch of excuses when the day's work is done, leaving the boss a brief-case full of problems to solve while you *waste* your brain energy! You're not paid to solve these problems???

Well, he who never does any more than he gets paid for, never gets paid for any more than he does. Whether you handle a pick or a wheel-barrow or a set of books, dig ditches, or are a housewife, still you must be occupied at something you love to do, in order to be happy.

"What are you doing here?" The first man leaned upon his hoe and complained. "I'm breaking my back, workin' thirteen hours a day in this beastly field." The second farmer said, "Me? Why I'm earn' three dollars a day." But the third tiller of the soil, looking out over the valley, smilingly replied: "Friend, I'm changing this barren waste into a garden of production!"

Are you "breaking *your* back," "Earning dollars a day," or planning and dreaming into reality the thing you love, and which you *know* will bring you Lasting Happiness? Are you changing your "barren waste into a garden of production?"

Are you producing a life of health, wealth and happiness?

You were meant to attract and enjoy a rich, abundant, full life. You can live a prosperous life when you call on the greatest power of the universe to aid you. You can receive counsel for all problems, and gain strength to overcome every weakness, and challenge you might encounter.

Some of us, like a magnetized piece of steel, can attract what we desire—others, and that includes, unfortunately the great majority, have this power of attraction only in a limited degree, if they don't lack it entirely. How, then, do you activate this power of attraction that is so essential for happiness?

This book explains how to mine the mind to attract love, happiness and abundance. It clearly demonstrates the means to develop attraction artistry.

The lessons here were developed from my personal experience of escaping from near poverty, and gaining prosperity. I was broke, deeply in debt and with substantial family financial responsibilities. I was in middle life with the doors of industry, and business closed to me since the demand was for younger workers. When I was so burdened with worry, I could only feel the terror of life, and my own weakness. It was a horror beyond horrors.

So, I went out on a lonely country road with the thought in mind that perhaps the short cut was the best way out. But, fortunately I concluded that it was the coward's way. Instead I would start out to see if I could find myself, and find the secret of that power which I had always felt stirring within me.

Well, at last I did find my True Self. I learned that to accept defeat, to think of life as a burden, to look upon it as hopeless, is to "play hooky" and run away from the very lessons which we are put here to learn. And the desire to escape from them or to take the "short cut," is to abandon an enterprise that, if carried to its incarnate completion, or the end of this cycle of experience, would yield values that are permanent in the soul's progress toward freedom. To quit would be like one who abandons a professional education that would have made him superior and independent, and thus force him to a whole life-time of menial work of an undesirable and unprofitable nature.

Since that lonely day on the dark, country road, I have learned treasured lessons that all the preceding years of suffering seem as nothing compared to the great things that have come to me since the day of my great decision. I am now enjoying supreme health, boundless joy, love and prosperity more than I could have imagined.

I wrote this book to help readers to navigate through the fog hanging over minds torn apart by conflict. It cuts through to the basic truths which are everlasting, and gives readers a lift to inspire and assist them. Health, happiness and prosperity can be yours when you put into practice the principles described in these pages.

The key to the mystery of manifesting money lies within this book. It explains how you can become the master of infinite possibilities by calling to your aid the greatest forces in the universe. It's a master-key that can unlock the inner secret chambers of riches. The Unseen Forces will lead you to great wealth when they know you will use it to help the World.

You don't have to be unhappy.

You don't have to be sick or lonely or poverty-stricken.

No matter how miserable the past has been, no matter how blank the future may seem, you can change it. The past can be wiped out and the future transformed! In whatever depths of degradation and despair you may be, however great your regrets or your fears, you can begin to be happy and prosperous right now, today this minute, *if you will.*

2

Money Cults

Some people worship rank, some worship heroes, some worship power, some worship God, and over these ideals they dispute – but they all worship money. **Mark Twain**

That Almighty Dollar

"How much is it worth? How much money can I get out of it? How much money do other people have? How can I get more?"

The general idea persists that money controls the entire world.

But, money isn't everything... or is it?

Some would argue that money is our modern society's true religion. The desire for it is not an inconsistent one. Money, to humanity, is the universal symbol of value. It represents power and freedom to the degree that it adds comfort and happiness to life. Hence, we must admit that we need and want it.

In itself money is nothing, however much the misers and hoarders of the world have been hypnotized by it, along with the business man whose only interest is its accumulation. When it passes that point, it becomes as great an affliction as poverty. The man who considers himself utterly ruined because he is caught in a financial crash which diminishes his many millions to half a million, is in the same class as the woman who recently allowed herself, her husband, and her child to starve while she had several thousands of dollars sewed up in a mattress. Both are based on the theory that supply is material only, and that, being limited in quantity, it must be snatched at, fought over and hoarded.

False Profits

The great god of the world is money. The temple of this god is dedicated to profit. The priests of this temple are the "money changers," commonly called bankers. Property is exalted on the throne of the temple, and life lies crushed at the foot of it.

While hearts are set on power and wealth and position and advancement, life is one long series of heart-burnings, jealousies and disappointments. Men fear and dislike those who might stand in their way or be preferred before they are.

It's well-known that the need for economic security, and power drives some men to overlook higher standards of conduct. In fact, a vast majority of occupants of prison cells today are there because of a need, or fancied need, for money. Get money, as life without it is not worth living, is the predominant idea nowadays.

To acquire wealth, men often ruin their characters, and women throw their lives away. For its possession they have stooped to dishonor; they have stolen and tortured and killed. For lack of it, they have taken their own lives. People will deceive, con or swindle for it. Any sacrifice is not too great for it, and it is this inordinate desire for false profits that causes countless failures and no end of misery, woe and suffering.

For most people, the difficult thing is to demonstrate money. Why do they so often fail in their demonstrations? In the first place they must clean their mental houses. They possibly have had impinged on their subconscious this thought: "Money is the root of all evil." This is not even a correct quotation of the full scripture, which is, "The love of money is the root of all evil."

To know money as part of original Spirit substance and to love it as such is to be absolute master of it—and when you say, "Come" it comes. It can and must be held in the thought: money as an obedient servant, as demonstrable Spirit substance. We are told over and again that we are children of God, and Jesus said, "All that the Father has is mine." But, only if your mental home is cleared.

In cleaning your mental house, be watchful that the creative subconscious is not clogged with such embers of negative thought as, "It is as easy for a camel to pass through the eye of a needle as it is for a rich man to enter the kingdom of heaven."

Many a benighted soul has remained poor thinking it to be a free passport into the mythical mansions. Now is the time for such persons to awaken from the sedatives of half-understood scriptures. They really need to "stir up the gift (creative power) within them," which is divinely reasonable by the teachings of the Bible. Certainly it's difficult for a rich man to attain true spiritual awareness if he holds his riches as a prophet or god, but it would be just as difficult for a poor man to enter the "kingdom of heaven" consciousness if his soul were seething with resentment, bitterness and greed.

Henry Ward Beecher once said, "The whole air is full of gold dust, and men see everything through its haze."

Most people have a false and exaggerated idea of riches. Poverty, unemployment and crime have come to light as direct results of a blind allegiance to this god of gold, which is the representation of a power that has been misunderstood and misdirected.

Money is but manifestation of energy and of such power that, unless we control and dominate it, we will find it like a very Frankenstein monster bent on our annihilation.

"If you make money your god, it will plague you like the devil," warns Henry Fielding.

It's a good thing to have money, but bad for money to have you. Wealth and opulence are all right when you do not make them your god and fall down and worship gold. Wealth should not be the master, but the servant of man. Honestly earned and wisely expended, it's a grand, good thing.

The wise people of the world, who acquire great wealth, are non-attached to their work and non-attached to their wealth. They work for work's sake and reward of their work is money. They expend it in a wise way; they use money for religion, education, the arts, the sciences and anything that has a tendency to refinement and culture. These people live in the realms of the soul and mind, and not in gratifying the senses—the appetites and passions. When persons live on the plane of pleasure alone, they live on the plane of pain and suffering.

When we live for the soul and mind, we receive happiness. Our spiritual and intellectual sides, when developed and equalized—harmonized—bring accord, peace, joy, bliss and delight. Then it is, and not until then, that we know how to master fortune and not be a slave to fortune. So, dear readers, it's a good thing for you to have wealth, and a bad thing for wealth to have you.

King Solomon, who had great wealth, drank deeply of every cup of sensuous pleasure, at the end of his earth life said of pleasures, "Vanity of vanities; all is vanity. I have seen all the works which have been done under the sun, and behold, all is vanity and striving after wind."

All the wealth of the world can't bring happiness to men who live for pleasure alone.

The story is told about the elder Cornelius Vanderbilt, with eighty to two hundred millions of dollars, who said to a servant just before passing out of his body, "I am poor and needy; yes, poor and needy."

The day after his death one man said to another, "Have you heard the news? Commodore Vanderbilt is dead!"

"How much did he leave?"

"He left it all."

Evangelist, Billy Sunday says, "Some are just in life for the money they get out of it. They will tell you north is south if they think they can get a dollar for it. They float get-rich-quick schemes and anything for money."

Ultimately money will master us until we master money. Why? Because like electricity, money is a force of nature. And just as we have faith that the lights will shine if we turn on the switch, we must have faith that money will flow when we flick the inner switch of faith.

God will overflow your cup, so grab the biggest one you can find.
Rob Liano

13

Prosperity is Divine Will

One of the ideas that is being replaced rapidly by a positive truth in religious thinking is poverty and lack are approved by God. The desire for abundance is a Divine urge within us. The longing is natural. Why then is the opposite believed? The grounds for this idea that a lack of sufficient supply is a virtuous state probably springs from several sources.

For thousands of years we have been told and believed: that we were born sinners and came into this life to suffer for those sins; that anything which caused happiness and comfort were evils to be shunned; that sin was our inheritance from Adam and Eve and there was nothing we could do about it.

Additionally, man has always justified his inability to demonstrate prosperity by saying that his lack must be God's Will for him. This is one source of mistaken belief in God's approval of lack. In spite of criticisms of prosperity, man's soul has not been discouraged in its quest for security, bounty, order and wealth—all of which, within himself, man has eternally believed to be his birthright.

In spite, too, of the apparent resistance to his search for prosperity, imposed by the suggestion that his search is unrighteous, man has looked eternally to God for his supply and support. David affirmed in the bible that, "The Lord is my shepherd, I shall not want." Jesus taught us to pray, "Give us this day, our daily bread."

As man looks about the natural kingdom, he beholds a kingdom of bounty and plenty. His logic therefore leads him to the inevitable point of knowing that God intends for him to be adequately supplied (as lavishly, profusely and sufficiently) as those things which he sees in nature.

These remarks can stimulate your thinking in at least two ways:

First, you can accept the idea with greater conviction than ever before that the lack and insufficiency in your life are not only unnecessary, but actually in opposition to God's plan and Will. It automatically follows that you will demonstrate money if you understand how to apply its laws correctly.

Secondly, the realization can be quickened within your thought that God is the one true source of that greater goodness.

God is Abundance

The Law of Abundance is real; it isn't a mere theory, nor a fable of the pulpit. It's the mechanical action between spiritual abundance and factual objectivity. The Law is unwavering, impersonal, impartial; it's ever ready to act, but it does not particularize of its own initiative. God is the Source of the richer supply that you seek. By turning in faith, believing in His power to prosper you, He finds channels thereby made available through which a fuller flow of His wealth may materialize in your affairs.

In increasing numbers, human beings are following the practice of turning thought to God *within*, recognizing Him to be the true Source of supply, and invoking His Presence in all affairs of prosperity and of all-sufficient wealth.

As you meditate, let it be with your eyes closed to all else, your body relaxed and your mind and heart open to the loving Presence, Provision and Power of Divinity within.

Faith Equals Fortune

If you feel this is a mean, restricted, harsh, unconquerable world of privileged minorities, you are judging exclusively by temporary effects—and stirring into activity more hardship. There are many unpleasant conditions in the world, but they do not need to continue forever. Each individual who turns to the Power Within for understanding and strength to pursue a right course adds impetus to a general forward movement, which must eventually bring this world to its intended likeness to Heaven.

You must have faith. I do not mean an abstract, vague feeling that some far-off power will drop your heart's desire into your lap. Faith is the electric power in you. Light, Heat and Power are yours when you have faith. Faith turns on the power when you say, "I Will."

There is power in mental work of faith, but it works in and through you. It does not do anything for you that it can't do through you. You can sit in a dark room all night with a light switch within reach, but unless you turn on the switch, you won't be able to see. You press the "I" button and fortune responds. It turns on your radiance in the morning when you say, "I am ready for anything." You will develop self-confidence in your own ability to grant your desires and make your dreams come true. It gives you warmth when you say, "I can do it." It sends vibrations out to people as you pass them so that their response is, "There's a woman who looks as if she could do anything she wants to do."

Faith or self-confidence brings about an attitude of expectancy. We not only expect, but we *know* that things are working together for our good. You can assume this attitude even though your faith is weak. Assume an attitude of opulence towards the world and you will begin to attract opulence. Little things will happen which will bring added richness into our life. You will start watching for them, and you will be amazed. This is the meaning of "to him who hath (a rich consciousness) it shall be given."

Regardless of your Will, however, the moment you lose hope and faith, your destiny is established like a bullet shot from a rifle which can't be turned from its course. As long as your optimistic hand holds opportunity, you govern "Fate." But if you drop it through pessimism, you are in the hand of Fate's "destiny" not your own Will. If you are skeptical about your own ability, your light will be wan. Fear puts a shade around each individual who allows himself to think or say I am not strong, not capable, not educated, not equipped, not sure.

People want to make instantaneous demonstrations, and often this is done, and we should never lose this perfect vision of our capability to make rapid demonstrations. But if we do not have instantaneous demonstrations, we should never fall into the slough of despondency and say it can't be done.

What stopped you from making your demonstration? Nothing but yourself. I grant you that potentially we are all capable of instantaneous demonstration, but if we haven't grown to that point, let us continue to speak our word of faith, nothing doubting. The positive, continuous, importuning prayer of a man who knows the law avails anything and everything he desires.

*Each soul is pregnant with its own potentialities
just as each light station radiates its own power.*

Soul Food

How many poor souls are beset with incessant doubts and fears as to the God-given power which is the rightful heritage of all—of even the lowliest of human creatures! In man's negative condition an awful dread paralyzes his efforts to better himself. We all have our moments of despair

17

and indecision, with a longing to tune in any direction for advice and sympathy; and yet, if we but knew, the remedy has ever been within ourselves—waiting to be called forth by right thinking—to heal our maladies, mental as well as physical.

The cry of agony, and oftentimes unavailing regret, that goes up from the suffering ones is heartrending. Yet the cause of all their misery is not hard to find, nor, happily, difficult to overcome.

You make your own environment, and you can surmount them if you Will. Are you weak in some particular purpose? Then let yourself be strong by using proper thought. Do you find you lack self-control? Then endeavor to strengthen the Will by unceasing effort. Are you, in spite of good resolutions, easily tempted to diverge from the paths of honor and righteousness? Then strengthen that part of your character by correct methods. Do not let your environment conquer you; YOU CAN CONQUER IT! It's all a mental attitude—whether your troubles arise in the mind or in the body. You can soon change conditions if you set about the task in the right spirit.

First, stop appealing to external influences—the objective side of life—for help. Advice is well enough in its way, but it can't compare to that which we get by a few moments' silent meditation with the Divine part of ourselves—the ETERNAL SOUL. It's within the reach of every one of us to acquire at least a fair share of happiness, let the conditions be ever so bad. We have spoken about this before elsewhere, and have given the remedy—RELAXATION OF MIND AND BODY, a perfect restlessness of the brain and flesh! And this can't be done by spasmodic effort. It must be rather the result of constant practice and regular action.

Following out these simple hints, be true to yourself and watch the results. Someday it will come to you, with the suddenness of a lightning flash, that happiness has at last arrived to reward your efforts, and you will scarcely know how it came.

Suffering ones! You who have all the needed forces hidden within yourselves (to promote your growth from unfavorable conditions), make the effort NOW—seek happiness as it should be sought, with a full and loving heart. Send out kindly thoughts to the whole world; harbor no malice, no enmities; be charitable and merciful to every living creature; speak not ill of anyone, and see nothing but that which is good in your fellows. THEN WILL THE VIBRATIONS OF LOVE RETURN TO YOU INCREASED ONE HUNDRED FOLD.

You will begin also to get glimpses of a mysterious and joyous change in your prospects, both in mind and body and worldly advantages.

One of the chief objects of life is to change for the better (by loving solicitude) all unhappy conditions in every walk of life—to console the sorrowing, to uplift the struggling soul to overcome all evil tendencies in self from your soul to all of the Creator's creatures!

Him Who Gives Gits

Do you know the time is coming when we shall become tired of the toys of material possessions and shall strive after some nobler, more worthy ideal, and in that endeavor we shall be as successful as we have in the attainment of material prosperity.

Until we have the courage to try it, we can never know the wonderful sense of freedom which comes when we stop trying to find happiness through grabbing and wanting. Realize that the secret to contentment is *giving*, not getting; seeking our own in another's good.

The happiest woman I ever met was one who was so interested in the well-being of others that she had ceased to have any desires at all for herself. She could never be disappointed, because she never expected or wanted anything from her friends except to serve them. She was never slighted because she was not interested in what people said or did to her, only in what she could do for them. She was not at all the popular idea of a saint; in fact, she was a bustling little woman with a very sharp tongue. But she learned the secret of a happy heart. Having lost her life in that of the world around her, she had found it again more abundantly.

Many people have the negative notion that generosity will impoverish them that unless they put a price on every service, only a meager compensation can come to them and keep the fearful wolf from the door. They are constantly on vigil to conserve forgetting that even an ungrudged drink of water will return as a blessing, as help when they are in need, or as supply overflowing into the door of some heart's desire.

A child of God finds unlimited opportunities to serve as His channel of good to others. Anyone who has the temerity to doubt the truth of this law has only to look around, and observe earth's successful, happy people. They are invariably lavished with gifts of one kind or another. Their lives are primarily dedicated to the service of mankind.

Time, talent, money, friendship and good cheer are all pearls of great price to both giver and receiver. We might easily paraphrase the famous command of the Master and say to those who seek success, "Go ye into the world—and give."

> Small kindnesses, small courtesies, small considerations habitually practiced in our social intercourse give a greater charm to the character than one display of great talents and accomplishments. **Light of Truth**

Give Whatcha Got

You can't shut your fingers together tight enough to hold water in your hand. Not only water, but you should give money or ideas or just work—or let all of them flow. Release your energy and let it expand and get to work. That is the only way you can turn it into money. That is the only way you can put life into your idea, and set it whirling to draw to you every means needed for its fulfillment.

Those means include—money for your living, money to further your ideas, money for very right purpose. But you must start it flowing by releasing what you have, whether it's money or ideas or any other form of energy.

Have you heard of the old hand water pumps that used to adorn most kitchens during the 19th and early 20th centuries? To start them drawing water, you had to pump to start the flow. The same is true for starting the flow of the energy of money.

Start the flow.

Give whatcha got. It's the support of Secret Givers that makes possible to bring sunlight into the lives of those who, too, long have known little but darkness. Sometimes their end may be achieved with only a few words of cheer or advice. Sometimes an article of clothing or furniture is needed. But whatever the need may be, no problem is ever considered hopeless, no plight insignificant. Always before the Secret Giver is the precept of the Master in whose footsteps he has chosen to follow.

Make this the happiest, most gladsome world possible, not only for your own dear ones, but for *all*—the lonely, the sad and the depressed. Radiate your own happiness and fully understand the meaning of peace and goodwill.

Waking Thoughts

Someone is sad—then speak a word of cheer;
Someone is lonely—make him welcome here;
Someone has failed—protect him from despair;
Someone is poor—there's something you can spare!

Thanks Millions

If you wish to receive wealth from the world, be grateful, be thankful for the many good things.

Dissatisfied minds hold attention upon the common, ordinary, inferior and thus become more and more ordinary every day. We gradually grow into the likeness of that which we think of most. The mind that dwells constantly in the presence of true worth is daily adding to its worth; it's gradually and steadily appropriating that worth with which it's always in direct contact. But it can't enter into the real presence of true worth, unless it fully appreciates the worthiness of true worth; and to appreciate anything, we must feel this deep gratitude whenever we have the privilege to enter its presence.

Take the ups and downs of life without a single murmur or complaint. Learn to take the bitter with the sweet, sorrow with joy, and never whine or grumble at anything. The person controlled by its content to work and wait, knowing that something better will come to him as soon as he is ready for it.

The grateful mind expects only good things, and will always get good things out of everything that comes. The good things that come to us come because we have properly employed certain laws; and when we are grateful we enter into more perfect harmony with those laws, and we are thus able to employ the same laws to still greater advantage. A child can understand this, and those who are not aware of the fact that gratitude produces that effect, should try it and watch results. It may be new to many that the attitude of gratitude does bring the whole mind into more perfect and more harmonious relations with the laws, energies and powers of life, but this is mathematically correct.

The course to purse is to cultivate the habit of being grateful for everything that comes; also give thanks always to the Most High, and feel deeply grateful to every living creature.

Knowing as we do that the more perfectly we apply the laws of life, the more we become, the more we accomplish and the more we gain possession of, we can't justly ignore the Law of Gratitude for a moment. Anyone who will do it can demonstrate it to be the truth.

Each has her own ideal of what life should be, and the measure in which she recognizes this ideal determines her success and happiness. We haven't been filled with desires without the means of satisfying them. There is need in the world for the best that each of us can give, and when we realize this and determine to supply that need, we have made a good start for a life of prosperity.

Remember giving is living. It isn't "what you have" that makes you successful. It's what you give; to others, to yourself and to your Creator.

When you realize the power of the Kingdom of Heaven within, you will no longer be subject to the whims of want of money. You will understand when the need for money arises: "Ask and ye shall receive. Seek and ye shall find. Knock and it shall be opened to you."

Know that *"every good gift and every perfect gift is from above, and cometh down from the Father of Lights, with whom is no variableness, neither shadow of turning."*

TEN COMMANDMENTS OF MONEY

Reverend Ike was affectionately called Dr. Money. And, like a doctor, he assumed the role of advisor and counselor for healing people of their financial illnesses.

In order to aid the process of healing, he formed Reverend Ike's Ten Commandments of Money to help millions of people to put their financial lives together. These commandments represent ten attitudes which can magnetize your mind about money. If you believe money is scarce and hard to get, that's exactly how it will be for you.

Study these commandments. Let them enter your heart and your subconscious mind, and they will work for you to eliminate your doubts and fears because as you learned, your mind is a magnet, and it will draw whatever you believe about money.

Reverend Ike's Ten Commandments of Money

From Dr. Frederick J. Eikerenkoetter II's classic
"Master of Money" audio lessons.

I.
Thou shalt not think that money is evil.

But rather, think and say: Money is totally good. My desire for money is totally good and right. I want and use money only for good purposes. Thank God for money!

II.
Thou shalt not speak evil of money. Thou shalt not say that "money is hard to get, or to hold." Money hath ears and will flee from thee.

Think and say: Money is wonderful stuff. I see and feel myself having and enjoying more money. I see money flowing into my life with ease. I see and feel money coming into my life in new exciting ways. I am open and receptive to new, honest money-making ideas. Thank God for money!

III.
Thou shalt do right about money.

Think and say: I am willing to do right about money. I have no need to do wrong about money, or to do wrong to get money. Thinking right and doing right about money draws more and more money unto me. I pay my bills with joy. I use money with joy. Money has no power over me to make me do evil. I have ALL POWER over money.

IV.
Thou shalt give right about money.

Think and say: I give money to good causes that I believe in. The money that I give becomes Money-Seed and is multiplied back to me many times and in many ways. I give regularly and with a system. Therefore, I am blessed regularly. My giving does not cause me to have less. My giving causes me to have more.

V.
Thou shalt not serve money, rather, money shall serve thee.
Think and say: I am not the servant of money. Money is my loving, obedient servant.

VI.
Thou shalt be aware that money loves thee, money loves to fill thy hands and pockets.
Think and say: Money loves me. Money loves to fill my hands and pockets. Money will not stay away from me. Money loves to serve me. Money loves for me to enjoy it. The more I use and enjoy money correctly, the more it flows into my life. I love money in its right place. I love the good that I can do with money.

VII.
Thou shalt not fear money, that it will corrupt thee. "Only the corruptible can be corrupted." If thy religion cannot stand money, then thy religion is bad – not money.
But rather, think and say: I have no fear of money. I am not afraid that money will corrupt me. Money cannot make me a worse person. I am a better person because I have money to meet my needs, to enjoy, and to share. Money is not against my religion. Money cannot come between me and God. I can serve God better with the convenience of money.

VIII.
Thou shalt not deny money. If thou deny money, money will deny thee. If thou art accused of having much money, deny it not. Never say, "I don't have any money," even if you don't. "Let the weak say 'I am strong.'"

Think and say: I make it my business to think, act, and look like I have money. I must become that which I say I am. Therefore, I boldly declare I AM rich! I see it and feel it. I AM rich in Health, Happiness, Love, Success, Prosperity, and Money.

IX.
Thou shalt see to it that thy money makes money, no matter how much or how little you have. Thou shalt have "Money Making Money!" Money loves to increase and make thee rich. Money shall work for thee.
Think and say: I see and feel myself having "Money Making Money!" I see myself having money drawing interest. I see money working for me; bring me more money in honest, exciting ways.

X.
Thou shalt not seek "something for nothing."
However, thou shalt make the most of the money.
Think and say: I realize that there is no such thing as "something for nothing." I avoid all offers that promise "something for nothing." Therefore, I don't get caught in losing deals. I realize that I cannot get "something for nothing" from God or man. I serve God by right thinking, right doing, and right giving. And I am rewarded "according as my works shall be." I serve mankind in my work – whatever it is. Life pays me according to my thinking, doing, and giving.

He is suffering from a disease known as lack of money.

3

Poverty is a Disease

Poverty is spiritual halitosis. **George Orwell**

Anyone who has ever struggled with poverty
knows how extremely expensive it is to be poor.
James Baldwin

It appears that there is a disease that is becoming more and more widespread among the masses. It's a dangerous disease: both biting and contagious. And it can be difficult to cure.

The disease of which I speak is poverty. Turmoil, pain, distress, unhappiness and calamity are its manifestations. The poor are bound by its chains.

Most of you probably know the general definition of disease: a structural or functional disorder in humans, animals or plants. But do you know that poverty is also a form of sickness? Actually, disease and neediness go hand-in-hand. Poverty can be considered as much a chronic illness as cancer, diabetes and cardio-respiratory disorders. These are illnesses of the body.

Destitution is a disease of the brain; a malady of the mind that is akin to addiction or other mental weaknesses. In fact, poverty is a mental disease that manifests itself in physical lack. Misfortunes of all sorts gather about the psychologically ill and the frail. Mental weakness produces malignant discontent, discordant strife, and clogs the wheels of progress and prosperity.

Before a cure of any disorder including poverty can be affected, we must first understand the cause and remove it.

Cause of Much Poverty

The disease of ignorance is the father, and mother, of all diseases. Persons who so suffer are responsible for such suffering, even though it appears the opposite is true. Fact is, they have brought it upon themselves in spite of thinking they do not attract it. They have created it all either by poor thinking or lack of thinking.

If you think that you are subject to poverty and lack, and if you think that only material means and human efforts can save you from these distressing conditions, then you are a slave to them. They are real to you, and it's impossible for you to escape from them. By your thoughts, and beliefs you bind yourself to negative conditions. But it's all a terrible mistake.

You are a slave only to your own thoughts.

You are not a slave to material conditions, in reality, except for your thoughts and erroneous beliefs. You are a spiritual child of Divinity living in a spiritual universe, and all your wants are supplied by Spirit. All the riches of the universe are merely a thought or idea in Divine Mind which is inexhaustible: therefore your supply is inexhaustible.

Your only limitation is your own thought.

So long as you think and believe that your supply is limited by bad trade, that poverty and lack can affect you, and that only bank balances and investments can save you from hard times, you remain in bondage.

Not only are you then liable to be limited, or even stricken by poverty, but your wealth, if you possess any, is a burden and source of anxiety to you.

Thus, the cause of poverty is pitiable thinking or lack thereof. A large part of mankind is in bondage to a feeble state of mind that clings to trouble and misfortune. They do not know how to attract the good things, but do with certainty invite failure. They are down in the depths of adversity and poverty because their mental attitude keeps them there. These minds are so clouded with error that they have no power to produce or create anything but a morbid atmosphere which poisons and stifles their lives.

In reality, false thinkers repel, drive away and keep away all success, all prosperity and all happiness. These folks become poorer and imagine the rest of the world is doing likewise.

We find exactly what we look for; this is the Universal Law. If we look for bad, bad will come to us. If we think weakness, failure and poverty, we certainly will get our full share of these ills.

Since poverty is rooted in ignorance, one who is impoverished is unaware of the true nature and relation of things. So long as we remain in a state of ignorance, we remain subject to poverty. We are deprived because we are not willing or prepared to learn the lesson it came to teach us.

A child who, every night when its mother took it to bed, cried to be allowed to play with the candle; and one night, when the mother was off guard for a moment, the child took hold of the candle; the inevitable result followed. The child never again wished to play with the candle. The lesson of obedience: it's one foolish act that the child learned and learned perfectly. It learnt that fire burns.

This incident is a complete illustration of the nature, meaning and ultimate result of poverty. As the child suffered through its own ignorance of the real nature of fire, so children of a larger growth suffer through their ignorance of the real nature of things that they weep for and strive after, and that harm them when they are secured. The only difference being that the latter case the ignorance, and the evil are more deeply rooted and obscure.

Manifestations of the Poverty Malady

According to Moorish Grand Master, C. Freeman El, poverty is your sin. Being ignorant of yourself is poverty, being sick is poverty. Melancholy is poverty. Being without love, happiness and romance is poverty.

There are a number of worrying beings who keep themselves continually disturbed and are in poverty by holding false ideas in their minds. They are impoverished because they feel helpless, and believe that their pitiable condition is an evil that must be endured. They accept their vulnerability and do not try to fight their deficiencies.

Some folks fail because they fear failure. They do not aspire to live their dreams because they believe they can't dwell in the lofty places in life. Rather than be disappointed that they tried and failed, they simply don't try.

Many others who would otherwise be prosperous readily accept the suggestion of helplessness, and make no effort to battle with the wave of oppression they imagine is bearing down upon them. There are those that accept their unhappy condition because they do not believe their surroundings are favorable for success. They choose to wait for the right time, the right event, the right this or the right that.

Too many people claim a very few are "born with a gift." Therefore, they make no progress towards fulfilling their dreams, and complain that they must be content with their lowly position in life because they were not born with the gift of wealth.

Let us not forget the great number of people that would like to be successful if they could do so without much exertion. They would like to go to sleep at night on a bed of ease, and awaken in the morning to find their brows crowned with laurels and their hands filled with gold. They want what they want when they want it, and how they want it. But this rarely happens even in this progressive age. Nothing yet has been found to take the place of aspiration and effort.

A life of ease, of financial security, free from worry and hardship is no test of character. It takes friction to do that. It takes overcoming trouble and worry. Anyone can continue courageously through life when all is serene, and the going is good; but it takes real guts to fight when the going is rough and seemingly hopeless. This is the real test of character and strength.

Could they but see that the poor in mind are getting poorer, while the rich who believe they will get richer are, indeed, getting richer, they would instantly see clearly and reverse or cleanse their minds, and become happy and prosperous.

We fully understand how hard it is to rouse the sick and poor, and get them to listen to the cause and cure of their misfortunes. But, there is a sure and permanent cure of poverty. There is not a person in existence who really desires to change his condition for the better that can't do so.

The moment you waste force or energy in fear, doubt and regrets is the moment you are in danger of poverty. But, being poor is corrective. It's remedial and is therefore not permanent.

Orison Swett Marden tells us "If all of the poverty-stricken people in the world today would quit thinking of poverty, quit dwelling on it, worrying about it and fearing it; if they would wipe the poverty thought out of their minds, if they would cut off mentally all relations with poverty and substitute the opulent thought, the prosperity thought, the mental attitude that faces toward prosperity, they would soon begin to change conditions. It is the dwelling on the thing, fearing it, the worrying about it, the anxiety about it, and the terror of it that attracts it to us. We cut off our supply current and establish relations with want, with poverty-stricken conditions."

Cure For Poverty

Since mental blindness is the cause of many forms of poverty, before a person can shake off the shackles of want, he must realize that success depends entirely upon himself.

Thus, the remedy for poverty is simple: right thinking. You must know the Higher Law of Abundance.

There is a higher Law of Supply than that obtained on the physical plane. In the higher Spiritual realm there is no such thing as lack or insufficiency. If this Divine sufficiency is not expressed in your life it's because your thought-life is wrong. So long as you acknowledge the power and supremacy of material limitations, and so long as you think from this standpoint, you are a slave to your environment, and nothing can set you free. Your liberty must come through the understanding of the Higher Law.

You must know that supply is as certain as the rising of the sun.

Students of Truth are not more anxious about the supply of their daily needs than ordinary people are about the rising of the sun. You would not lie awake all night being consumed with anxiety concerning the fate of the sun. You go to sleep and think nothing whatever about it, for you *know*. You know that you live in a universe of perfect order, governed by Perfect Law and that the sun must rise; so you don't worry.

Your understanding banishes care.

In just the same way the spiritually illumined *know* that their supply will manifest just as surely as the rising of the sun; therefore they don't worry. This is the only care-free life—the life of complete dependence upon Divine Harmony, based on understanding.

Convince yourself that there is no reason in the world why you should not be prosperous and happy. Believe that there is no power except yourself that can hold you down. Breathe in courage and hope with every inhalation. Send out thoughts of your success with every exhalation.

In other words, rouse the tremendous hidden powers of self. Men and women with the elements of greatness in them do not let environments or circumstances control their lives.

35

They recognize the Divinity within them and assert with the indomitable Napoleon, 'I make circumstances.'

Free from all fear of the return of adversity, this method can secure permanent prosperity. Through this process by the disease of poverty, or any adverse condition or circumstance can be put on one side never to return.

Undesirable conditions can't check the advance of one who is determined.

To obtain opulence one must become conscious of his own power, and determine to be the master instead of the slave of circumstances. You must believe that you are of use in some way; that you have something important to offer the world. A hopeful, determined attitude must become a permanent one. No one can climb out of the pit of poverty by taking a firm hold one minute, and sliding back the next.

So we say, for a preventive and cure of poverty, you must:

Reverse Your Thoughts!

Unhappiness, misfortune, failure, the loss of money can be the greatest good fortune that could happen in our lives, could we but understand it. Innate and hitherto unused and unsuspected **power** is called out by failure and misfortune. Originality, courage and tenacity are developed only by courageously meeting misfortune and failure.

Get to Work and Love it

Much shortage comes to Money Mad people; people who desire to get rich quickly without effort. The cure for scarcity is labor. Effort is essential to happiness. Learn to work with gratitude and be engrossed with the idea of the good your work will do rather than with the thought of how much money you can get out of it.

The secret of success is "Be of Worth." Do something of worth and create something that has worth.

When you have worth, the world will want you; you will be in demand. When your work has worth, your service will be in such great demand that you will have more opportunities than you can take advantage of. When your products and services have worth, you will scarcely be able to supply the demand. These are facts and being facts, all attention and all personal power should be concentrated upon the cultivation of worth.

Do work you love.

Develop your hobbies into money-making ideas.

Do what you love.

No matter how old your body is, it can do some work if your mind is willing to get relief from poverty.

No matter what your environment may be, keep your purpose ever in mind. Accept cheerfully whatever comes to you, resolving that it shall in some way help you on the goal of your ambitions. To cure poverty, you must *believe* what is an absolute fact—that you are in use in some way; that you have something valuable to offer to the world. When you have something of value to give to the world, the world will come and get it without being forced. Everybody is looking for the new, the better and the superior; and if you have it, announce the fact.

Advertise it.

Be always active in your own affairs, and waste no time or energy in meddling with the affairs of others. No matter what happens to you, keep a cheerful and hopeful mind, and you will eventually succeed beyond all your fondest expectations. Health, success and happiness are always abundantly measured out by the higher, and unseen powers to those who are persistently patient, hopeful and courageous.

Fire to Aspire

A few at the top are crowned with health and success, and it's their mental attitude that placed them there. Thus, this cure for poverty suggests to an open and aspiring mind the TREMENDOUS POWER of the WILL, which can do wonders if intelligently exercised. Anyone, with a little mental effort, can train and develop the Will just as easily as we train and develop the muscles by persistent physical exercise. The moment we fully and vitally realize who and what we are, we then begin to build our own world.

As long as one thinks he is weak, that he is a poor worm of the dust and that he has no chance, that his fate is to be whirled hither and thither by forces and powers over which he has no control, just that long he will be at the mercy of negative forces. But I tell you, everyone can accomplish grand results the very moment he cleanses his mind of fear and doubt about his ability to succeed.

AS A MAN THINKS SO HE WILL BE. Continually think disease and you will continually be weak and sick; continually think poverty and you will continually be poverty stricken. These are *absolute* truths.

We must strenuously strive to be SOUND, HELPFUL and SENSIBLE; we must be strong, self-reliant, self-supporting and not dependent.

Poverty is a sin that can't bring happiness.

To abolish poverty we must work with faith and hope and banish once and for all any and all fears of failure—worry about the past or apprehension about the future. We must live intensely in the present, let go the past and the future will take care of itself. WE ARE ALL MASTERS OF OUR OWN FATE.

Let me repeat; we must first think wealth and then use the mind to discover the true foundation of wealth. The mind, in its search for the cause of wealth, will soon discover that the well-directed energy—action—is back of all wealth. But along with this energy we must have faith and courage.

This is a busy world, and we are living in a wonderful age of large undertakings and great progress. Nothing stands still. There is no backward movement! The world is better and busier today than it was yesterday, and will be better and busier tomorrow. It's the calm, honest, thorough, thoughtful, and busy workers who make this condition of growth and progress; not the worrying, hurrying, fretful, gloomy, morbid, pessimistic minds who persist in looking at things through the wrong end of the telescope. No one will be successful, or feel the glorious good times which are here to stay, unless you are hopeful and cheerful and willing to play the part to assist in the advancement and happiness of this world.

And so, when poverty comes, that is not the time to sit down like a coward and quit, that is the time to keep moving courageously and persistently. We must expect to meet obstacles; then we are not unprepared for them. We accept them as strengthening, and not as retarding influences.

Never Ever Give Up

As we have discovered, all our sufferings are due entirely to a lack of knowledge and wisdom. Now, my sole aim in writing this cure for poverty is to wake people up out of the delusions in which they live. I will continue to plead with poverty-stricken men and women, to rouse within them their mighty forces to overcome poverty and drudgery. I tell you all, you are greater beings than you imagine you are; your dormant or latent powers, and forces are great and wonderful. YOU and YOU alone limit yourself, and suffer because you won't rouse yourself to the grand truths which wise and good people have taught for thousands of years.

How, then, shall you direct your effort? What will defend you, protect you and lead you to the place of peace, power and plenty? We go over and again all the lines of failure and success and, at last we stumble, sometimes almost blindly on to the Law.

Keep the idea of abundance always present in your consciousness. If one plan fails, try another and another and still another, but do not quit. You are not defeated no matter how often you are trampled, until you lie down spinelessly and quit. Nature abhors the cowardly, the cringing and beaten quitter, the weakling who refused to try again because he failed, once or a dozen times, or a thousand times.

Adjustment of self is the secret of happiness and opulence, not the adjustment of your circumstances because once you adjust self, your circumstances will naturally be adjusted. The second is the result of the first; together they are cause and effect.

Remember, no matter where we find attainment and success, we can be sure that we will find back of these arms of power which men call Thought Force. When we remember that the back of everything in the world is the Thought Force that produced it, we need not hesitate long in choosing the weapons which alone will lead us on to conquest.

Poverty is not an abstract something outside yourself; it's an experience in your own heart, and by patiently examining and rectifying your heart you will be led gradually into the discovery of the origin and its nature, which will necessarily be followed by its complete eradication. When we fail to evolve from this state of poverty of mind, body and soul, to an enriched consciousness and an abundant life, we fail to fulfill the Creator's intent and purpose in having created us.

We will now realize that the word "poverty" is really a misnomer. There is no such thing as poverty. There is ONLY power! Power to meet all your needs; power to create the infinite riches you demand of life; power to give you the intelligence you need to meet all your needs; power to give you the perfect body, and to keep it in perfect health; and power to supply you with the money, food, shelter, clothing and luxuries you desire.

The only demand made upon you by this Infinite Divine Intelligence is that you recognize the Divine Power back of apparent poverty and pay homage to that Divinity.

It's the Way of Liberty.

4

Hundred Million Dollar Club

*If something (such as money) is going to affect your life,
it's best to know as much as you can about it.*
Donald Trump

I have had all the disadvantages required for success.
Larry Ellison, Millionaire

Everyone wants to prosper. The entire world loves the prosperous. Americans are expressly proud of their self-made. These people blasted their own way out of the prison of poverty and lack of opportunity that confined them, and then fought for every bit of position they achieved on the ladder of success. These people show evidence that adversity and temporary failure are blessings in disguise.

Some of the richest, most successful people started poor and unknown. In sacrifice and struggle, they paid the price for wealth and fame. Handicaps provided them motivation to become successful. Such folks give concrete proof that this world is one of unlimited opportunity.

A multi-millionaire said "The great fact of life of power, of commanding triumph, lies in the knowledge of the secret forces that dwell within the human brain and body. The men who win the world's wealth, recap its luxuries and enjoy its comforts, are those best familiar with the hidden forces within themselves, and whose knowledge pertains to the use of those powers. By them, and them alone, have men risen to the world, and their education may be great or little."

The greatest oak was once a little nut that held its ground.
Author Unknown

Cash is the Message

An outstanding example of a man who prospered from preaching prosperity is an extraordinary clergyman surnamed Eikerenkoetter. This old Dutch name represents acorn planter or carrier, aptly describes Dr. Frederick J. Eikerenkoetter II's rise from poverty to affluence. Also known as Reverend Ike, he was a teacher of extraordinary qualities, a truth leader of world renown. As his name suggests, this great and fearless soul developed from a tiny acorn into a mighty oak tree.

While other preachers denounced desire for material wealth on earth, Rev. Ike's theology was in sharp contrast with this message in both practice and substance. Preaching a unique form of the gospel based on wealth, he teaches, God gives us innate power to gain health, happiness, love, prosperity, good fortune and unlimited wealth. His God is loving, kind and generous; an all-powerful God that dwells in each of us. Through this power we can overcome our financial struggles, and live a wealthy, productive life "here and now."

Beware, he warns, of the Money Rejection Complex. "If there is the slightest suspicion in your mind that money is evil

44

and dirty, this will form a Money Rejection Complex." Rev. Ike taught that the LACK of money is the root of all evil. He was drawn to ideas that originated with New Thought because they placed greater power, and responsibility upon the individual to affect the course of his or her life in this world rather than suffering now, and praying for a better life in the hereafter.

In the stillness of your meditation, he guides, in the stillness in your mind, instead of saying money is evil, say "Money is totally good. My desire for money is totally good and right. I want to use money only for good purposes. Thank God for money."

Often called the "diamond-studded disciple of health, happiness and prosperity," the mainstream press pegged him a fraud because of his extravagance. Known for his bold declarations as, "You can't loose with the stuff I use." Rev. Ike answered his critics claiming his philosophy works well and helps a lot of people. He held, "We're successful, prosperous and rich and I make no apologies for it. My wealth proves my philosophy is effective."

Rev. Ike inspires millions worldwide. More than 2.5 million people followed his broadcasts on over 1770 radio stations and television appearances. One of his telecasts was called *The Joy of Living*. Ordinary people over the world: black, white, rich, poor, famous movie celebrities, political figures, sports champions, religious leaders gathered to hear his message.

His ministry receives heaps of letters. All were answered with special words to charge their lives with these blessings: good health, happiness, love, success, prosperity, good fortune and unlimited money.

Right Here and Right Now!

Ike's unique philosophy, the *Science of Living*, is a form of positive self-image psychology and positive self-motivation that teaches when a person believes in himself, confidently and correctly, this motivates him to "be what he wants to be, do what he wants to do and have what he wants to have; right here and right now."

As he assures us, "If the stuff I use doesn't work for me, I have no right to give it to other people. If my message does not prosper me, I have no business offering it to anyone else. Positive self-image psychology works and causes people to be successful right here right now." And, truly, it worked for countless people.

One of his most important messages is his philosophy will not work for those who will not work with it. "Believe in yourself." He says, "Spiritually and mentally lazy people don't want to use their own mind. My stuff will not work for that."

If you desire money, try his money mantra, "I like money. I need money. I want money.... Money is not sinful in its right place. Money is good."

When you try this with faith, soon you will see the money starting to roll in.

> I am no longer cursed by poverty because I took possession of my own mind, and that mind has yielded me every material thing I want, and much more than I need. But this power of mind is a universal one, available to the humblest person as it is to the greatest. **Andrew Carnegie**

From Poverty to Power

Andrew Carnegie, a Scottish-American industrialist, who gave away five million dollars a day, began his career earning

$1.20 a week. Think about this folks, a boy who earned two cents an hour grew an empire worth more than four hundred million dollars by his strong will and integrity, not only became one of the richest men in the world, but also one of the kindest-hearted philanthropists.

Born in 1835 in Dunfermline, Scotland, Carnegie's parents were too poor to afford a doctor or midwife to deliver him. Life was tough for this family that lived in a simple home where his father ran a weaving business. They cooked, ate, and slept in a tiny, dark attic.

When the Carnegies moved to America his father peddled tablecloths door-to-door, that he made while his mother worked sixteen to eighteen hours a day washing clothes and stitching boots for a shoemaker. Although the family lived in poverty, Andrew possessed a tough spirit and determination. He often told his mother that he would be rich one day, and so, rolled up his fortune with uninhibited drive. In 1901, he sold Carnegie Steel Company to JP Morgan for $480 million which equates to $310 billion in today's dollars.

Carnegie loved making money because he had a mission before the end of his life. His spirit was simply searching for a new challenge which would benefit others. He fulfilled his self-imposed duty by giving away nearly all of his gigantic fortune.

The quality of the philanthropy reflected the man himself. There was a huge and sentimentally-administered fund to which access was to be had on the most trivial as well as the most worthy grounds. And there was the side of Carnegie's giving that concerned itself with great ideals. There were the famous libraries—3,000 of them costing nearly 60 million dollars. There were the Carnegie Institutes in Pittsburgh and Washington, Carnegie Hall in New York, the Hague Peace

Palace, the Carnegie Endowment for International Peace, and his precedent-making Carnegie Corporation of New York.

Some of his happiness was spent in pursuit of wisdom. He would spend his time receiving instruction and reading and writing systematically.

His 1889 article, *The Gospel of Wealth*, stimulated a wave of philanthropy by calling on the rich to use their wealth for social improvement. Carnegie wrote that "the fundamental idea is that surplus wealth should be considered as a sacred trust to be administered by those whose hands it falls, during their lives for the good of the community."

Before his death in 1919, Andrew Carnegie gave about almost 90 percent of his fortune, about $350 million, to foundations, charities, universities and libraries.

He said that it was his strong desire or will, persistently and firmly held in one direction that made him succeed.

The medicine of the future will be music and sound.
Edgar Cayce

Love Saves the Day

Self-described "musical host," and dance culture pioneer, David Mancuso, rose from poverty to opulence by revolutionizing New York City night life. In doing so, he contributed to the social revolution of love, peace and harmony.

David brought to the world the era of disco music and disc jockeys, with his weekly Saturday night dance parties at his downtown loft.

The Loft combined music and dance in a cool retreat for creative types; all adding to a sensual experience of freedom.

At a time when the struggle for civil rights movement reached a high point, the Loft offered a hint into what true community, democracy, and unity were actually like. It was a kind of utopia where his "guests," who were multi-racial, young and old, straight and gay, rich and poor, singles and couples, came together to create a positively-charged atmosphere. As such, the Loft was not a disco. It was an experience. It was a feeling. The Loft represented a changing era: personal and social change.

In their book, *The Record Players: D.J. Revolutionaries*, British journalists, Bill Brewster and Frank Broughton, called David the most influential figure in night life history. "David," they wrote, "brought to his Saturday night gatherings the values of the 1960s counterculture, an audiophile's fascination with sound technology and a voracious appetite for all styles of music."

Born in Utica, NY on October 20, 1944, his mother left him in an orphanage two days later. David's happiest childhood memories revolved around a nun called Sister Alicia. He remembers her creating "a happy place" for the children. She hosted parties that welcomed people of all ethnicities and classes. Colorful balloons flooded the parties. Music was modern and exciting as Sister Alicia encouraged dancing and fun.

David left the orphanage to live with his mother in Utica. At sixteen years of age, he dropped out of school to work as dishwasher to finance his move to Manhattan.

In the city, he held a few odd jobs, but struggled to pay rent; so he hosted a rent party a 647 Broadway and called it *Love Saves the Day*, sent invitations and sold tickets for $2.50 for his first party on Valentine's Day in 1970. It was a remarkable success. Sister Alicia's parties matured into David's Loft. By year-end, the parties were so popular, all of the people who showed up couldn't jam in, so he had to choose his guests.

Mancuso told Professor Lawrence of University East London "I remember when we had the first blizzard and people walked from over the Brooklyn Bridge."

The Loft offered non-judgmental freedom. It was a safe, intimate space to relax with friends and meet people. Giant balloons and bubbles floated seemingly with the music. Tables were spread with exotic food. Huge pillows were strewn against the walls in the main dance room where you could lie back and relax. Here minds were altered, and lives were forever changed.

Mancuso described music in spiritual, mystical terms to journalist Vince Aletti. He said he was inspired by "listening to birds, lying next to a spring and listening to water go across the rocks... there were times when it would be intense, and times when it would be very soft."

He seemed to believe that music had magical powers. And he made many of us believers in magic!

David's aim was to meld into the music, and allow its power to transform the guests. Responding to the energy of the crowd, he "orchestrated a seamless, interruption-free wave of sound, with an integrated light show, in an uninhibited, colorful, environment that lasted until dawn."

For $2.50 you could come in relax, eat, dance and party. "I wanted a situation where there are no economic barriers, meaning somebody who didn't eat that day or only has a few dollars in his pocket can eat like a king... drinks are included." He continued, "There's no difference if you have a lot of money or a little."

The Loft was a cultural revolution. The parties provided the model for dozens of clubs to come, notably the Paradise

Garage and Studio 54 in Manhattan and the Warehouse in Chicago; and they decisively influenced the culture and musical styles associated with them, from disco onward.

In essence, the Loft reflected Mancuso's belief in love as a guiding and universal principle. "The Loft is a feeling," he said, "a kind of mystical experience."

The parties represented the sixties dream of peace, liberation, love and diversity. As David told the Japanese newspaper, Yomiuri Shimbun, "I always like music, and I always like bringing people together."

> If you love it enough, anything will talk with you.
> **George Washington Carver**

Not Just Peanuts

Local farmers called him "the plant doctor." He was George Washington Carver of Tuskegee Institute. Born a slave, Carver, who was a self-educated tireless worker, investigator, scholar and scientist. He became fascinated by plants, and developed hundreds of products. Peanut products produce plastics, dyes, paints, cosmetics, soap, ink, wood stains and gasoline. Sweet potatoes yield flour, vinegar, molasses, postage stamp glue, rubber and gasoline.

A heartfelt believer in prayer, he humbly held:

"It is not we little men that do the work, but our blessed Creator working through us."

He believed that all possess creative power. Putting his hand on the bible he said, "The secret lies in here, in the promises of God. Those promises are real, but so few people believe that they are real. If they would only believe!"

Because of his great love for all things beautiful, it can be truly said of him that he found "tongues in trees, books in the running brooks, sermons in stones and good in everything."

Glenn Clark, in his little book, *The Man Who Talks with the Flowers*, said of Dr. Carver, "This old gentleman who always had a flower in his buttonhole and love of God in his heart, gave America a message, a service and a life that were not only unusual and remarkable, but will always be permanent. His influence will go on forever."

Shortly before his passing, Dr. Carver predicted a great spiritual awakening in the world that will come from plain, simple people who know—not merely believe—that the Creator answers prayer.

George Washington Carver was a successful scientist, inventor, and agriculturalist, but success to him was not measured by the usual methods. He said: "It is not the style of clothes one wears, neither the kind of automobiles one drives, nor the amount of money one has in the bank that counts. These mean nothing. It is simple service that measures success."

The remarkable achievements of this humble man have been described as a practical reaffirmation of the American principle of freedom of opportunity for all alike.

Sweet Success

An American chewing gum company, Wrigley's, was founded on April 1, 1891 by William J. Wrigley Jr. based on his philosophy to offer customers a little "something for nothing."

David V. Bush, author of *How to Put the Subconscious Mind to Work,* tells of how this extraordinary man, who was born in Philadelphia, moved to Chicago in 1891 to pursue a career as a soap salesman. He noticed that the stick of gum he gave away as incentives to buy his products were more popular than the merchandise for sale. Consequently, he directed his energies toward producing his own lines of gum. He started with two flavors, Lotta Gum and Sweet Sixteen Orange.

During the economic depression in 1893, he introduced Wrigley's Spearmint® and Juicy Fruit® gums. In 1907 he risked all he owned to launch a massive advertising campaign. This daring move skyrocketed his company into national prominence, and set the stage for his company's future groundbreaking advertising strategies.

Initially, success was not sweet for Wrigley. Making his way from the ranks of the dollarless to the heights of the wealthiest, he faced plenty of loss along his journey. Twice he went to New York City to sell his gum, and twice he went broke. It's said that New York chewed him up, chewed up his money, chewed up his advertising, and then spit him out.

His second failure sparked a champion's determination, "I am coming back to New York and when I do, New York will know I am here!"

Although he left New York temporarily defeated, he did return. Wrigley came back with a victorious attitude, and the spirit of a conqueror. His advertisements concentrated on bill boards and in magazines and newspapers of the city; and Wrigley won back the two fortunes he had lost in New York. He made a million, and then another. His fame spread, his gum was chewed and chewed and chewed all over—even New York was now chewing Wrigley's gum.

During his company's rapid rise, Wrigley Jr. became one of the nation's leading supporters of employee rights and benefits. In 1916, he created health and welfare departments in his Chicago factory in addition to establishing minimum wages to provide his employees with financial security during the Great Depression. Wrigley was also one of the first companies to grant his work crew weekends off. Recognized as one of the champions for supporting programs that benefit the company and the communities it serves, Wrigley's provided more than $70 million to non-profit, worldwide organizations and communities since 1987.

Today Wrigley's continues to make a difference for the people, and for the planet. Its global operations span more than 50 nations to distribute products to more than 180 countries.

What about you? Can you handle defeat? Do you possess the courage to get back up and win? Your future depends upon how you answer these questions.

Lessons from Masters of Wealth

Perseverance. It's the very hinge of all virtues. Generally throughout the world, the cause of nine parts in ten of the hopeless failures which occur in men's undertakings and darken, and degrade so much of their history lies not in the want of talents, or the will to use them, but in the vacillating and aimless modes of using them, in flying from object to object, in staring away at each little disgust, and thus apply the force which might conquer any one difficulty, to a series of difficulties so large that no human force can conquer them.

The smallest brook on earth, by continuing to run, has hollowed out for itself a considerable valley to flow in. The wildest tempest overturns a few cottages, uproots a few trees and after a short space, leaves no mark behind it. Therefore, honor the virtue of perseverance. Without it the rest are little better than fairy gold, which glitters in your purse, but when taken to market proves to be slate or cinders.

Fear of failure, or lack of confidence in one's ability, is one of the most potent causes of failure. You, who expect to gain success in the world must make up your minds that, come what may, you will succeed. You must make a firm conviction that you were made for success, that success is your birthright, a right of which you can't be deprived by any combination of adverse circumstances. Hold in your mind the thought that success is as much your right as the acorn has the right to become an oak, or the rose bud to become a rose.

Failure, like disease, is abnormal. Nothing is more depressing than holding for years the thought of defeat or that you are unlucky, and are not intended for success as others are.

We often have the chance to test the boundaries of our ability. Out of effort and resistance comes power. We should embrace this opportunity to live our lives to the fullest. We can accomplish pretty much whatever we make up our minds to accomplish. If we are not forced to test our strength, through dire-necessity, through struggle, through hardship, we seldom discover our possibilities. Lay it down as a general rule—and a sound one at that—that real strength comes from struggle, hardship, adversity and handicaps imposed upon us by causes beyond our immediate control. If we could "control" these causes they would not exist because we would eliminate them, thereby depriving ourselves of the most beneficial experience that can come to a human being.

The greatest artist in the world could not paint the face of a Madonna with the image of depravity constantly held in his mind. You can't expect to be loved if you surround yourself with an atmosphere of hatred, envy and jealousy; and for the same reason you can't succeed if you surround yourself with an atmosphere of doubt. So, Aim high. And don't be scared.

The cave you fear to enter contains the treasure you seek.
Joseph Campbell

5

Are You Scared?

Money is the headache and money is the cure.
Terri Guillemet

Worry is meditation to the wrong god.
Anonymous

Are you scared? You are not alone.

Some of our worst enemies have been fear. We fear illness. We fear failure. We fear of poverty. Indeed, a man can go through all the horrors of war, and yet kill himself rather than face poverty.

The American Psychological Association's *Stress in America* survey tells us that that Adults reporting "extreme stress," increased from 18% in 2014 to 24% in 2015. The usual finding during 10 years of the survey, is that stress is caused by three primary factors—money, work and the economy.

When you stop to think of it, it's now true that the average person's life is governed by constant fear of financial troubles. Too many people allow themselves to be dominated and overwhelmed by constant fearful thoughts of destitution and misfortune, thereby yielding to such suggestions as: "What if my efforts should prove unfavorable?" or, "What if I should fail?"

Failure today is fear advertised.

All such weakening and character-demoralizing thoughts, anticipate and manifest disaster. Indeed, since one of man's greatest fear is the fear of failure, he is afraid to attempt more than his daily routine tasks, for fear he won't be a success at something greater. Perhaps he wins an advancement at his work, but his fear of the added responsibility almost takes on human form, staring at him with cold, unflinching eyes, driving him surely back to his old job again. Many a talented man has hesitated to strike out for himself because he had not courage enough to overcome his fear of failure.

Millions upon millions of people have killed themselves with worry; fretted to death by their antagonism to the conditions in which they lived, and for which they found no remedy. They died of *fear* nursed in their own breast.

Fear is the strongest instinct handed down to us by our primeval ancestors. It may be our greatest handicap. This emotion was originally given to us for protection. It was and is a blessing. Animals use fear to escape or destroy their natural enemies. Humans have it to avoid lightning, volcanoes, earthquakes, floods, prowling beasts, and other dangers.

Civilized man, however, have multiplied its terror a thousand-fold and often senselessly.

What one of us is free from these defects? The following worry story warns of its perils.

There is an old account of a man who one day on the highway met the ghastly, hooded figure of Plague.

"Where are you going?" he demanded.

"To yonder city," Plague replied, "to kill a hundred people."

And he passed on.

A few weeks later, the same man met Plague coming back from the stricken city. "You lied to me," the man protested, "in yonder city, thousands lie dead."

"Nay I killed the hundred, as I said. My twin brother Fear killed all the rest."

How true it is that fear—or worry—is responsible for so many of our troubles, real or fancied. The truth is that the most deadly instrument for marring life is fear. When the mind pictures the monstrous or the evil, the imaging faculty itself is misused; while thinking in general is given all sorts of false and disagreeable patterns.

Fear demoralizes the spirit, destroys character and ambition. Fear induces or causes diseases, poverty and misfortune. Fear paralyzes happiness and prevents success. The more people I see, the more convinced I am that fear causes more misery than anything else. It has not one redeeming quality. It is all evil. It chains the brain.

Brain Chains

What are these brain chains?

Does your mind entertain thoughts of fear, sickness, poverty, unhappiness—do you lack courage—have you been hampered in reaching your success goals?

Brain chains are weakening and character-demoralizing thoughts that anticipate disaster. Too many people allow themselves to be dominated, and locked down by constant fear restraints, and yield to such suggestions as: "What if I should fail?" or, "What if my efforts should prove unfavorable?" Like shackles, irons and chains bind the body, doubt and fear can bind the mind.

Fear, worry and anxiety—and the various members of their families, are most persistent of the undesirable emotions. These are the things which break a person down. They may go on brewing for years before their effects are finally noted. A fit of anger is exhausting too; but the anger is usually over in a few minutes. Nonetheless, our fears are always with us wearing down the mind like the proverbial drops of water which wear away the stone.

We hardly realize the extent to which fear has crept into our lives and language. We even say, "I'm afraid I can't agree with you," or "I'm afraid it's going to rain." Many people are afraid of interviews, strangers or anything new. These constant fears sap our energies and exhaust us. They drain the nerve-cells of their vitality.

Instead of the nervous system working like a well-oiled machine, it begins to grate upon itself, like two files which are rubbed together. Mental and physical work are then performed with greater difficulty. The subject begins to *drive* himself, to make himself work; and this depletes the nervous energies still further. The time finally comes when he must take a complete rest—*or* have a nervous breakdown.

He is then *forced* to take a rest.

Author of *The Coming Science*, Hereward Carrington, tells us that anyone who has undergone a "nervous breakdown" will tell you that it's the most fiendish mental torture imaginable; that a broken arm or leg is not to be compared with it; and that almost any other physical illness is to be preferred. One of the reasons for this, doubtless, is that it's very "close to home." It affects the mental life, it arises from some unpleasant experiences. They become part of our mental equipment, and as we grow older they color our judgment much like dye colors water, and anything that does that causes grave anxiety.

What are the causes of fear? How can it be prevented? And how cured? These vital questions we must answer in turn.

It's the emotions which cause the trouble. These can be our arch-enemies. All negative emotions are exhausting. They seem to "short-circuit" the nervous system, discharging the stored-up energy of the nerve-cells in very much the same way that a battery may be discharged, and its pent-up energy released. We all know from experience how exhausting strong negative emotions can be.

When the Mind is Blind

In these states, you are in a form of myopia, or nearsightedness, that exists which blinds you to all but the physical facts and factors in disease. We know of the existence of the invisible substances that we call molecules, but we do not seem to understand the unseen and un-seeable substances that we call thoughts. We believe in the agency of microbes, but do

61

not seem to consider the agency of mental microbes—the little devils of lust, anger and jealousy and doubt. We believe in the body's reaction on the mind, but not in the mind's reaction on the body. And we certainly do not believe the mind attracts or repels fortune.

When the conscious mind worries, the subconscious mind is thrown out of harmony, and consequently fails to perform its functions properly.

Two defects that blind the mind, Worry and Fret, abide with us all, to a more or less extent. These two guests, in a while, will get such a hold on the mind that it's almost impossible to get rid of them.

> **WORRY** and **FRET** were two little men
> That knocked at my door again and again;
> 'Oh, pray, let us in but to tarry a night,
> And we will be off with the dawning of light.'
> At last, moved to pity, I opened the door
> To shelter these travelers, hungry and poor;
> But when on the morrow I bade them adieu,
> They said, quite unmoved, 'We'll tarry with you.'
> And, deaf to entreaty and callous to threat,
> These troublesome guests abide with me yet.'

Self-Pity & Worry & Trouble

In addition to worry, another false state of consciousness of which you must beware is Self-Pity.

It is a truism to say that, "It's no use crying over spilt milk." No one would dream of weeping over something that may happen in the future, and nothing in the past is worthy of tears.

A thinking writer has beautifully covered Self- Pity in these following four verses:

BEWARE OF SELF-PITY

It is not wise to take the view
That a malign and scurvy fate
Has now resolved to make of you
A special object of its hate.

The forces that give impetus
And destine us to lose or win
Are not the things outside of us
But rather those that are within.

We need not inert and numb
Beneath some unrelenting Chance.
All men of spirit may become
The architects of circumstance.

Self-pity is an atmosphere
That's deadly to a man's morale.
Let all foreboding disappear;
Convert "I could" into "I shall."

However grave your mistakes may have been, they give you no cause for regret if they have left you wiser than you were before.

Thus the philosopher realizes that in reality all tears are shed in moments of conscious, or unconscious, Self-Pity.

There is a well-known little book which deals with Eastern Philosophy, and declares that, "Before the eyes can see they must be incapable of tears," which means really that you can view life sanely, and wisely only when you have learned to eliminate your own small personality from the forefront of your vision.

When you have removed this stumbling-block to clear sight, you can appreciate both light and shade. As a wise Truth Student, you will keep both light and shade, knowing that there cannot be one without the other. You will, in other words, see things in their right perspective; which is to say that you have acquired a proper sense of humor! And if a sense of humor is not a passport to a happy and well-balanced life, then what is?

Self-Pity and Worry seem to go hand-in-hand, and it's so easy to worry about Worry! And it's easy also for me to talk to you of worry as if it were some sort of venomous beetle on the floor requiring nothing more than a heavy foot to put it out of existence. But, then, Worry *is* just some sort of venomous beetle of the mentality requiring a firm stand by the sufferer.

Trouble and Worry go hand-in-hand. And Trouble is something that many fail to escape, no matter how you try to avoid it.

Some get Trouble in big—and some in little—doses. Only Worry has the habit of making even the tiniest troubles into mighty big ones that threaten to grow so large—in imagination, mark you—that they seem to completely engulf you.

You must be firm with Worry, and realize that Worry never yet solved anything—and never will. It only begets more Worry, and those who are its wretched victims simple "double trouble, and trouble others, too!"

Trouble, after all, presents a problem to be solved. Trouble is a crisis to be met and passed. You must examine it as coldly as possible. You must see it in its true perspective, and contrast it against the true background, and not the background of a fearful imagination. Then sit down, and map out a course of action. Be practical and sensible. Be positive—not passive and negative. If you will do these things you will find that the thing you were worrying about has ceased to be.

Let's suppose there was a man in your house, an ugly intruder disturbing your peace and endangering your freedom. Would you sit down, and hold your head in your hands and do nothing—but worry? Of course, you wouldn't! You'd do everything in your power to put the intruder out, and send him about his business.

Well, Worry is just such an intruder of the mind; an ugly mental intruder, threatening your peace of mind, and even in extreme cases, sanity itself.

First, get to know your Worry, for the unknown is a fearsome thing. Then try to oust it, by joyously anticipating the thing you want, instead of the thing you fear will come to pass. This plan of action never fails. It's strange how when you boldly face your Worry—the trouble causing the Worry—there is very often the discovery that there is nothing really worth worrying about at all.

Love, understanding and a staunch friendship—these are wonderful allies when you are fighting worry. And always keep alive in your thought the fact that even the darkest day has its "tomorrow," a new day, filled with new hope, new striving, new faith; and an opportunity for new health, happiness and prosperity.

Let these defects become useful this very day—by knowing that peace is yours by casting them out of your mind forever.

Fear is a plant not of His Kingdom, and therefore it needs to be uprooted. Fear begins always in the self. If the self is adequate to meet ordinary circumstances, there will be little fear. But when circumstances are extraordinary, the self needs more confidence.

Because each man's fear is created in different circumstances, each requires a little different technique in stamping it out. This technique each man must develop for himself; and there is no fear that can't be trampled out if you will only set your foot upon it.

Analyzing fear, you will find it to be a simple thing—it is merely a mental state, nothing more. What you fear another does not, because his mental constitution is different from yours. If any other person can be without fear of a certain thing, you can adjust your mind in the same way. As long as fear is just an attitude, however deep-rooted it may be, to be rid of it you have only to supplant it with another state of mind. To imagine the evil is to impress the evil upon the mind; and a mind that is filled with all sorts of evil impressions can't attract fortune. Muddy water is not pure water even though it does, at times, flow peacefully in its own channel.

The impressions that are formed in the mind lead to thoughts, and thoughts lead to tendencies; therefore, the more evil the mind imagines, the harder will it be to remain on the path of prosperity.

Train the mind to constantly imagine the good, the true and the right. Study the daring.

Learn Courage from the Courageous

Reading biographies of great lives is a good way to stimulate your mind to the necessary action of booting fear out the same door it came in. Most great men "got that way," because through their struggles to overcome lesser fears, they developed the courage to tackle great problems, and live for great ideals. Edison did it; Schumann-Heink did it; Booker T Washington, Helen Keller, Harriet Tubman, Theodore Roosevelt and countless thousands have done it.

You can do it too!

Medal of Honor Recipient and American Fighter ace, Eddie Rickenbacker, said *"Courage is doing what you're afraid to do. There can be no courage unless you're scared."*

The opposite of worry and fear is faith and constructive imagination, and the mind will accommodate the positive thoughts of these as well as the negative thoughts of worry, but not at the same time; so why should one worry, when there is faith and constructive imagination?

"As soon as the fear approaches near, attack and destroy it." This quote by teacher, philosopher, economist and royal advisor, Chanakyaqu, more than once has driven fear of failure from my mind. At a time when I have been discouraged, when I have been afraid to go on, these words have come into my mind, and I have known that I must not let fear turn my head.

Maybe you will find a favorite passage of Scripture or quotation of some great person that you can use in the same way. It supplants fear with a forceful mental atmosphere.

Perhaps one of the greatest methods for overcoming fear is by the use of prayer. With a prayer on their lips, ordinary, fearful men of all races and religions have performed superhuman deeds of valor. Turning to a greater power, we tap the Supreme Source of Power, a dynamo of mental energy with which to overcome fear. We are able, by this means, to uproot those parasitic mental weeds: Fear and Worry and Self-Pity. In its place will rise the sturdy, divine eternal oak—COURAGE.

Courage is very roughly the mechanism involved. The question therefore is: how may we develop courage? What steps should be taken to avert the unfortunate finale of fear?

The answer to this question has been partly suggested in what has been said above. However, further details are desirable:

In the first place, plenty of rest and sleep are absolutely essential in order to replenish the exhausted nerve-cells. Ten or twelve hours of sleep a night are not too much for a person verging on a nervous breakdown. Relaxation exercises are very beneficial. The subject should consciously relax, many times each day, and as she walks along the street she should say to herself: "Relax, relax, relax!" This coupled with deep-breathing exercises, will prove very helpful.

Only that which is within us, which is in the mind, can disturb us. No external thing can gain a hold upon us. All defects, all defilement, all disease and poverty arise from the heart and mind. Freedom comes in a great measure by no self-condemnation and by *knowing* All is Good.

Discover Your True Self

To develop strong fortune, eliminate all negative states of mind, such as fear, worry, depression, and discouragement, lack of self-confidence, lack of push, instability, indifference, inertness and negativity in general. But there are additional ways that can free you from the bondage of suffering caused by pain or fear.

There is a sleeping lion in every normal human being. The challenge is arousing it. It's just a question of something happening that will awaken us, stir the depths of our being and arouse the sleeping power within us. Hold poise all of that power.

As Marden tells us, "...when we discover that we are more than mere bodies, when we at last become conscious that we are more than human, that we are gods in the making, we shall never again be satisfied to live the life of common clods of earth. We can never be timid, weak, hesitating or fearful. We shall feel a new sense of power welling up within us, a power which we never before dreamed we possessed and never be quite the same again, never again be content with low-flying ideals, with a cheap success. Ever after we will aspire. We will look up; struggle up and on to higher and even higher plans."

When we go out into the world, we are never again satisfied with a cheap success, with our old nature or are we content with our old environment.

Worry, like a rocking chair will give you something to do, but it won't get you anywhere.
Vance Havner

Fear is an Enemy – Shatter the Shackles

Are you afraid to meet people? Then go out, meet as many people as possible and talk to them. You will suffer at first, may say or do the wrong thing, but before long this fear will be conquered, and you will wonder why you were so shy. Is there a special problem which frightens you?

Face it. Don't run away.

Many problems dwindle when we meet them head on—but loom more menacing if we run away.

It's a grave insult to the Almighty to go around demonstrating negative qualities when we were intended to be sons and daughters of the Infinite! We need to stiffen our backbone, brace up our resolution, stand without flinching, determine to triumph over difficulties, and assume constantly an indomitable spirit of courage.

It's healthy to:

- Fill your mind with cheerful pictures.

- Teach yourself the cheerful art of living.

- Avoid worry. Learn to relax.

- Find a quiet spot in a comfortable position. Rest.

- Release your troubles, real or perceived & calm down.

Additionally, learn to gain the power of concentration of thought and hold steadily to the idea of serenity. Do not allow fear pictures to get a mental grip. Dwell not on sickness, failure or unhappiness. Substitute thoughts of health, success, life, gladness. Give love and kindness, even if apparently repelled. It can be done and it works! It's a beautiful gift to yourself to enjoy the present, and get a measure of happiness out of your immediate surroundings. Look upon each day as a small section of eternity.

Dark thoughts hurry along the inner processes of destruction.

Mind Masters suggest: At night, when you get into bed, relax the entire body, breathe deeply and gently, focus your thoughts steadily, and persistently on the good you want for the next day.

Repeat these words: "I have courage, faith, and vision to succeed in all things worthwhile. I have inflexible determination and iron will."

State what you want to become, and end up with: "I shall be what I want to be." Repeat the same process in the morning.

Drive out of your mind all negative thoughts. They cause the imagining faculty to weaken and deteriorate. Charge yourself with thoughts you want to encourage, because the mind is a power magnet, and attracts to it the things you constantly dwell on.

Two opposites can't be carried in the mind at the same time. Understand courage-confidence, bold self-assertion, self-faith are attributes of Divine Power. When this mighty force is cultivated in the performances of deeds which are noble and true, right and worth-while, sincere and honest, you really become God-like. And this consciousness of power (not egotism) commands respect.

Determine right now to overcome the serious deficiencies in your mental make-up. Cultivate a splendid self-faith; resolve that your life will be crowned with hope and happiness and fear is an illusion.

> Some of your grief you have cured,
> And the sharpest you still have survived;
> But what torments of pain you endured
> From evils that never arrived."

Now that the shackles of worry and fear have been removed, while anxiety and frustration eradicated, we can practice the art of manifestation with joy and understanding.

These lessons taught me how to rule all of my emotions. They showed me how to banish all of my fears forever.

I am no longer afraid, and now eagerly look forward with the keenest pleasure whenever I'm called upon to address an audience. Indeed, through my books, classes and lectures, I have been instrumental in helping many people to overcome fear to gain success and happiness. Instead of being timid and tongue-tied I have an increased fluency of expression and generate tremendous stores of magnetism when speaking before the largest gatherings.

I am now very financially free, emotionally secure and supremely happy.

I've mentioned these personal facts to assure other sufferers that they, too, can overcome this miserable repression, and acquire the *courage-confidence* they long for, just as I did. I now look eagerly to the future with knowledge that I will continue traveling the road to success and happiness.

Listen to the wisdom of Francis Larimer Warner, "As the sun cannot shine into a dark cellar when shut out, so wealth cannot flow to us individually, when shut out by our doubts and worries, and belief in lack as the reality."

When you let flaming inspiration guide you, you will have a passport to a happy and well balanced life.

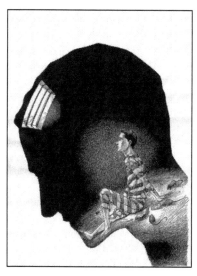

Men are not prisoners of fate, but only prisoners of their own minds.
Franklin D. Roosevelt

6

MindCraft

The mind is the master over every kind of fortune.
A great mind becomes a great fortune.
Seneca

The true preparation for wealth is in the mind. One's mind is the passkey to riches. It unlocks many doors, and we must utilize it with caution, for Chamber of Horrors as well as sunlit rooms of great beauty are there. Self-knowledge should be the goal of our quest and sincerity the staff that we carry though the shadows. We shall have to man our forces. Our weak resistance to the onslaught of dark, night-mare illusions, can't be tolerated if we are to rule our own lives.

73

Ignorance is responsible for all imperfection: ignorance of the underlying principle governing natural law. Science, united with Devotion, that Divine Principle, will remove those obstructions from the path of life and ultimately shed light upon the apparently incomprehensible Law. Our minds should be clear and free, open and ready for our soul's instructions. The only path to this perfectly modeled passkey to life's storehouse of wisdom is daily adherence to the principles which promote self-analysis, self-discipline, self-reliance, self-government and self-expression.

The material for the key is contained in the commonplace routine of daily living, systematic arrangement of harmonious thoughts and deeds, their outward expression of self-unfoldment through understanding of our own and others' deeds: tolerance, patience, kindness, service and love.

Dramatize & Demonstrate Your Heart's Desire

Every great person of genius who has contributed to the good of humanity, has held the completed picture of their ideal constantly in mind. Edison had a mental picture of the incandescent light, and made literally thousands of experiments before he succeeded in his invention. The great captains of industry saw thousands of wheels turning, mentally, before the ore was brought from the iron mines to make them. Sikorsky saw multiple-engine airplanes and helicopters in his mind's eye, before he built them. So you, too, may craft your own world from the things to which you give your attention.

You will find it to be an immutable law. You pay attention, and your attention will pay you dividends, large dividends. You have an ideal, a definite goal you wish to attain. You may think it's just a dream, maybe a "pipe dream," but if you hold it persistently enough and *start doing something about it*, it will start moving toward you, and you will be amazed at the speed, and ease in which everything seems to fall into place. There is a definite technique to the process which people use, either consciously or unconsciously, but the results are the same: *success.*

Remember, there is no one to tell you that you can't have your heart's desire, except yourself. But you must craft your mind, and attend to your attention.

MindCraft

MindCraft reveals the truth that real decision is always followed by action, or that action is an essential part of all real decision. But, what is the most powerful thing in the world in this age when everybody is seeking power and more power; power without limit.

We are more or less familiar with the power of the wind, steam, gasoline and electricity, but some of our modern investigators tell us of a remarkable power which they say may be available soon. They say, "there is enough of this wonderful power in a silver half dollar, if it could be released and if it could be harnessed, to drive one of our great ocean liners across the Atlantic from New York to Liverpool, and then back home again, and even then the power from this one little coin would not be all used up."

In other words the atomic power in a half ounce of silver, is as great as the steam power which can be produced from hundreds of tons of coal.

But amazing as are the wonders of atomic power, there is a power resident in each of us to a greater or less degree. This power is even greater than atomic power.

You are All-Powerful Mind, and your body is the instrument which is at all times expressing the exact activity of your mentality. Your mentality created your body, and still governs and controls it. You are master. Your body is servant. A healthy body can only be the expression of a healthy mind; likewise a sick body can only be the expression of a sick mind. The secret of creating a healthy body is to learn how to create a healthy mind. Similarly, an impoverished condition is the expression of a sick mind; opulence results from healthy minds. This is the power of your personal Will. Key here is to use your will to win.

How to Develop the Will to Win

There are seven essentials of the Will-to-Win.

First, if we would have the Will-to-Win we must learn to CHOOSE WISELY. You may ask, what does choice have to do with the Will? Very much, for just as a ship is helpless at sea without a rudder, so helpless is the Will that is not directed by wise choice. By your choice, you give direction to your Will.

Choice is not chance. Wise choice means that we must think the matter through seriously, and then make our decision. When you have made your choice, you should by all means stick to it; long enough at least to prove the wisdom or folly of your decision. Many of us are inclined just as soon as a thing gets a bit hard to throw it up, and change for something different. By all means change your mind, and change it frequently, if there is a sound reason for doing so, but otherwise you should stick to your choice.

An excellent example of this truth was once given when crossing the Atlantic in a terrific storm. The ship was in no little danger. To the novice it looks so simple for the captain to just change his course a bit, and go before the wind in a southwesterly direction away for the fog and icebergs.

He held on course.

Even though the ship failed to make her port, she could run to the safety of some more southern port, where in some quiet harbor she could ride out the storm, and then on safe, smooth seas she could later steam on to her destination. The captain, however, knew better.

He held his course.

Even though the waves rolled high and washed aboard, he held doggedly on. When he saw a tempest coming that he feared the ship might not be able to weather, he just hove to and heading up into wind, stood by for a time until the worst was over. And when he thought wise, he turned round to his course again, and proceeded as best he could. The wisdom of the captain was proved by the fact that the ship arrived safely in her destined port only a few days overdue.

Some of you may, this very minute, be considering the possibility of changing your course. By all means do so, if there is good reason for it. But if, as in most cases, you wish to change your course simply to avoid some difficulties, *Don't Do It*. Stick to your course, and see it thru, even if it's hard. You will come out captain of your own life, which is better than being captain of a ship, or even of a sports team.

The next essential is to MANAGE YOUR MOODS. The sea yonder, as far as we can tell, has no control over its moods. It's now lashed to fury by the tempestuous stormy winds, and now it lies with peaceful, mirror-like surface in the stillness of the early morning. The sea, for all we know, does not have consciousness, and so cannot control its moods, but we have consciousness, and that means power to control our moods. You should manage your moods, therefore, and the manner in which you manage your moods determines the measure of courage and success you possess.

Some folks think that a person who has a violent temper has also a strong Will. This does not follow. Temper is not Will. The Will is always controlled, and directed by reason; the temper is not. Temper is a mood that masters the man, but Will is a power by which the man masters his moods.

You do not feel like studying, and you have a test tomorrow? Well, too bad! Of course you can't study unless you feel like it. But what are you to do? What do you usually do? Neglect your study? Do not do it again; just manage your mood, and make yourself *feel* like studying.

Next, if you would have the Will-to-Win, you must HARNESS HELPFUL HABITS. You know we are all creatures of habit. Almost everything we do is done as a matter of habit, and with little effort or thought. It's easy to do anything we are in the habit of doing. Can any of you remember so far back as to recall how long it took you, and how hard it was, to lace your shoes for the first time? If it took you as long to get dressed now as it did then, you would not be able to get to school or work on time in the morning—some of you. But now these acts are performed quickly, easily and without thought because they have become habit.

If we will just use this natural tendency to form habits so that they will help us, we will have a tremendous undreamed-of-power at the direction of the Will.

A great many people will say, "Oh, I have no use for this Will business. I have tried it again and again, and it simply will not work." Such people are doomed to failure simply because they are working against the tide of natural tendencies. They think that this matter of Will is a question of just clinching the fist, and setting the teeth, and just going at a thing with grim determination. But the Will does not work in that way.

The natural way for the Will to work is like raising a vessel that is dunk deep down under the water, and into the ooze of the ocean floor. The way it is done is by getting large pontoons, and passing heavy cables down under the wreck, and up to the pontoons. Then, when everything is made fast in this way while the tide is out, the workmen can just stand by with folded arms, as old ocean comes in, and with an irresistible force begins to lift the pontoons and tug and strain at the cables, until slowly and silently and surely the vessel obeys the command of the ocean. It rises gradually up out of its bed on the ocean floor, and up thru the water as far as the tide goes.

Just so, if we will harness helpful habits to work for us, we will have an amazing power at the direction of the Will. When you think of habits, think not so much of harmful habits that drag you down, but rather of the helpful habits that help you to rise. And if you have not enough of such habits, just form them, for you surely can.

Again, if you would have the Will-to-Win, EXPECT MUCH OF YOUR LIFE. Be very bold, and expect all that is good and noble; the very best things you can think of.

So, expect much of your life and your life will not disappoint you.

The fifth essential of the Will-to-Win is to HAVE SOME WORTHY IDEAL. All people can be divided into just three classes: the lifters, shifters and drifters. The lifters are always by word and action advancing every good cause to the best of their ability. The shifters are always shifting their responsibility to others. And the drifters are content to be carried along by the efforts of others. Are you one of the shifters or drifters? If so, get some ideal at once.

So many of us are on the way, but we don't know where we're going. It is just as though you were to go to the railroad station and ask the agent for a ticket. And when he asked you where you were going, you should reply, "Oh, I don't know, most anywhere."

I think you might get a ticket to the insane asylum or someplace like it.

But, how much like that are we in regard to the great journey of life. Where are you headed for? You were all in high school and, of course, in due time you hoped to get a diploma; but what were you aiming at? What is it all for?

We should each have some ideal, a worthy one if possible, but perhaps most any ideal would be better than none at all. One young man in this country, some time ago, made it the ideal of his life to make people laugh. He cultivated an irresistible funny way, and went into the movies, and has made millions of dollars just being funny. He has been a success because he has had some goal; some ideal.

It's a difficult matter to present the next essential of the Will-to-Win. Perhaps you will understand, however, if I say it's necessary to GET A SELF-STARTER. You know just about how much a second-hand automobile is worth when it has no self-starter? The person without one is not worth much either.

It was a great improvement when they put the self-starter on the automobile, but it would be a much greater improvement if every person could just be equipped with one.

Just how can one get a self-starter, you ask?

Poverty, for some, is one kind of a self-starter, but there are many other kinds such as love, anger, pain, duty, pride, etc. But there is a far better self-starter. It has painted the world's greatest pictures, it has guided the chisel of the world's greater sculptors, and it has written the greatest poems, and composed the masterpieces of music. It has in all ways rendered humanity the very greatest service.

Find that self-starter, and your life will surely reach its highest fulfillment. Do you ask what this self-starter is? It could be told in a single word, but you would not understand. *The Other Wise Man* by Henry VanDyke found it though he failed to find the king, and each of you may find it if you Will.

Finally, the seventh essential of the Will-to-Win is to ACCEPT THE CHALLENGE OF A GREAT TASK. "Nothing to do." "Business is very slow." How often we hear such expressions: when all the while the trouble is with us, and not with general business conditions.

Have you heard of Louis, the paper boy, who can find something to do? Why cannot we? Who is Louis, the paper boy? Well, he is really not more than half a boy, and yet he is every inch a man. You see Louis lost both legs over twenty-five years ago; yes, they're both almost entirely gone. And every morning when you pass a certain corner in Boston, you will always see him selling his papers. He said the other morning that on the twentieth of next April it will be twenty-five years that he has been selling papers on that corner. In summer's torrid heat and winter's sleet and cold, day in, day out, you will find Louis there selling his papers.

No, it may not be much. Perhaps you would scorn such a job, though I will wager you would not scorn Louis' bank account, not one of you.

The point is this: he has been doing something. And here are we, all well and strong, with nothing to do. But we must do something for this age won't tolerate inaction.

It's the person who does things that are of advantage to his fellows who should be remembered and praised by posterity. Fifty years hence, when an unbiased history of these days shall be written, it will be the person who has done most to serve his fellows who will receive the greatest attention from the historian.

The idler, whether rich or poor, will be forgotten. So we must all do something, not only that we may be remembered by posterity, but that we may ourselves find the greatest joy in life. The happiest life is always the life of service.

But we must do more than that.

We must do the impossible, for that, after all is the real glory in living. "What," you say, "do the impossible? That cannot be!"

And then you begin to tell about the limitations of the Will. Of course the human Will can't at a single bound leap to the heavens. But, it can mount the ladder round-by-round by patient unremitting toil until, at last, we have gained heights which at first were impossible of attainment.

For the most part, the limitations of the Will that bring good endeavor to an end are those limitations which we ourselves have set.

We can, if we will, each do the impossible, or at least, that which we and our friends think is impossible for us to accomplish.

After all, that is the one thing in life most worthwhile for any of us.

In summary:

LEARN TO CHOOSE WISELY,

MANAGE YOUR MOODS,

HARNESS HELFUL HABITS,

EXPECT MUCH OF YOUR LIFE,

HAVE SOME WORTHY IDEAL,

GET A SELF-STARTER, and

ACCEPT THE CHALLENGE OF A BIG TASK,

...and you will have the Will-to-Win.

Change Your Mind – Change Your Life

Mind Masters through history tell us that, this is the real key to life, "if you change your mind your conditions must change too—your body must change, your daily work or other activities must change; your home must change; the color-tone of your whole life must change—for whether you be habitually happy and cheerful, or low-spirited and fearful, depends entirely on the quality of the mental food upon which you diet yourself."

Wisdom, they teach, won't allow us to waste time complaining about circumstances, problems, obstructions or difficulties in life. Wherever we focus our thoughts determine how we feel. If we have a bad disposition, we can't be healthy or happy. We can't be prosperous if we are sulky or surly or cynical or depressed or arrogant or frightened. We may feel that life can't possibly be worth living if we have sour attitudes. Unless we are determined to cultivate a good disposition, we may as well give up all hope of getting anything worthwhile out of life. And it's kinder to tell you very plainly that this is the case.

In short, if you want to make your life happy and worthwhile, you must begin immediately to train yourself in the habit of thought selection and thought control.

Mind Your Mind

New Thought spiritual leader, author and lecturer, Emmet Fox, describes the scientific way to *Alter Your Life*, and being in accordance with the Great Law.

It can't fail.

Now the important secret is how you can learn to mind your mind, and change your life.

First, he says, you must devote your mind solely to the task of building a new habit of thought, and during that time, let everything else in life be unimportant as compared with that.

Focus.

Concentrate your energies much like the concentration of the sun's energy when using a magnifying glass to ignite paper. Concentrate on developing wealth and abundance in your life. Concentrate on being rich; having all you need.

Fox also offers treasured tips for changing your life quickly. His guide, *How to Change Your Life in a Week,* says the most important of all factors in your life is the mental diet on which you live. According to Fox, the mental diet consists of food, in the form of thoughts, which you furnish to your mind. This determines the whole character of your life. Thoughts allow you to think, and the subjects that you allow your mind to dwell upon, make you and your surroundings what they are.

Everything in your life today – the state of your body, whether healthy or sick, the state of your fortune whether prosperous or impoverished, the state of your home, whether happy or the reverse, the present condition of every phase of your life in fact—is entirely conditioned by the thoughts and feelings which you have entertained in the past, by the habitual tone of your past thinking. Moreover the condition of your life tomorrow, and the next week and the next year, will be wholly conditioned by the thoughts and feelings which you choose to entertain from now on.

Fox tells us what happens is that when you apply the Law, conditions change spontaneously. You can't change conditions directly – you have often tried to do so and failed – but go on the SEVEN DAY MENTAL DIET, and conditions must change for you.

This, then, is your prescription:

The Fox Seven Day Mental Diet

For seven days you must not allow yourself to dwell for a single moment on any kind of negative thought. You must watch yourself for a whole week. You must not under any pretense allow your mind to dwell on any thought that is not positive, constructive, optimistic and kind.

You may start it any day in the week and at any time in the day. But, once you start you must go right through for the seven days. That is essential. The whole idea is to have seven days of unbroken mental discipline in order to get the mind definitely bent in a new direction once and for all.

Note this carefully. It's not the thoughts that come to you that matter, but only such of them as you choose to entertain and dwell upon. It does not matter what thoughts may come to you provided you do not entertain them. It's the entertaining or dwelling upon them that matters.

85

The thing to do is when a negative thought presents itself—tune it out. Turn away from the newspaper; turn out the thought of the unkind letter or stupid remark, or what not. When the negative thought floats into your mind, immediately turn it out and think of something else.

A perfect analogy is furnished by the case of a man who is sitting by an open fire when a red hot cinder flies out, and falls on his sleeve. If he knocks that cinder off at once, without a moment's delay to think about it, no harm is done. But if he allows it to rest on him for a single moment, under any pretense, the mischief is done, and it will be a troublesome task to repair that sleeve.

So it is with a negative thought.

Now what of those negative thoughts, and conditions which are impossible to avoid at the point where you are today? What of the ordinary troubles that you will have to meet in the office or at home? Such things won't affect your diet provided you do not accept or fear them, by believing them, by being indignant or sad about them, or by giving them any power at all. Any negative condition that duty compels you to handle won't affect your diet.

And, finally, remember that nothing said, or done by anyone else can possibly throw you off the diet. *Only your own reaction to the other person's conduct can do that.*

If you will follow his guidelines, then that week will be the most significant week in your whole life.

This is the estate of attainment to which man may aspire on this earth plane: the power which he may unlock within his own consciousness, if he will but accept nature's challenge to explore the mysteries of the universe: to transmute the limited poverty consciousness to the unlimited power consciousness.

Mind-Over-Money

It's important to know that you are a supreme creator.

You can craft your dreams of money by mapping out your imagination. Your mind. You must choose beliefs, feelings, and actions to support your vision.

Start now! Dare to explore the depths of your soul, and find the treasure chest within to help you to realize your dreams for creating prosperity and abundance.

A destination, like a dollar, is a matter of digging.
David V. Bush

7

Mine Your Mind

All riches have their origins in mind.
Robert Collier

More gold has been mined from the brains of men
than has ever been taken from the earth.
Napoleon Hill

Your mind is both marvelous and mysterious. True, the study of contemporary psychology is pervasive; its advances in theory and application are comprehensive. However, hardly enough effort has been made to study the mystic side of the mind. This is probably because the average person believes only what can be experienced through the five senses: sight, hearing, taste, smell and touch. Humans believe that because they can't see, hear, taste, smell or feel something, it's not there. To them, anything beyond the basic senses doesn't exist. Power of the super senses are instantly ridiculed, or dismissed as fantasy.

Yet, despite limited beliefs, the mind is limitless, and akin to magic. It houses great treasures, contains extraordinary mysteries, and can open the door to new, unexplored worlds. The power of your mind is awesome, and requires mining much like extracting precious gems, and other treasures from earth.

The awesome power of mind, and the hidden gems within are awakened through mining the mind.

It's a startling fact that once uncovered, the subconscious mind can act as a catalyst for wealth and happiness beyond imagination.

Let us take a little voyage of discovery.

Close your eyes, and imagine yourself floating out through space to the most distant star that has been discovered by our most powerful telescope. What would you find? You would be in a maze of starry heavens just as grand, and beautiful as the one we are gazing upon from this point in the constellations.

Powerful lenses in modern telescopes have revealed infinite stars. And many have worlds revolving around them. Our galaxy, the Milky Way, contains 100-400 billion stars and is estimated to have at least 100 billion planets. But this is only our expanse of the heavens. Astronomers tell us that the expanse of heavens is infinite... never-ending. The average mind recoils before such a stupendous maze, and the brain is stultified in an attempt to grasp such gigantic propositions.

Limitless riches are all around you. They are as vast as the universe and infinite as the stars. And since material wealth appears outside of us, many assume that the key to gaining riches is outside as well. But if you will open your heart and explore within, behold, you will discover that the source of this great treasure is within you.

Now repeat this trip, this time exploring your universe within. If you will study your own spirit and its limitless powers, you will gain a greater secret than any alchemist ever held; a secret which shall give you whatever you desire.

The great thing man has ever done has not been to discover the stars, but to discover Divinity within.

God has provided us with unconditional love and the power to attract indescribable, eternal happiness.

That secret is hidden within.

Think of your body as the jewel box, your mind as the silk lining and your spirit as the gem. Keep the box burnished and clear of dust, but remember always that the jewel within is the precious part of it.

Spiritual masters throughout the ages have proven that we must look within for the answers to our heart's desire.

Think of yourself as on the threshold of unparalleled success. A whole, clear, glorious year lies before you! In a year you can gain health, fortune, restfulness, happiness!

Push On! Believe! Achieve!

Each success in elevation not only increases the quantity, but also the quality of the energy developed. Higher levels of mental energy not only produce more quantities but also better qualities. And as qualitative effort increases, power increases.

As examples of this higher level: read a profound book in a field somewhat beyond your normal reading. It appears difficult at first and quite tiring but after you have passed the difficulties of comprehension and finally begin to understand, then you finally "catch on." Your tolerance of the subject becomes easier, and no longer is it beyond your mental grasp. The process is slow but sure. The boring must continue until the higher level is reached.

If you haven't acquired enjoyment of great music, go to a symphonic concert. Hear an orchestra. At the start, it may be difficult for you to grasp its meaning. But recurrences can carry you beyond the point of crisis, and then suddenly you find clarity. You find yourself taking a deep interest in it. Eventually you become a music lover because music says something you feel but can't tell.

And so it becomes increasingly important, as we go on in life, to penetrate the higher levels of energy. Those who never go beyond the surface levels do an injustice to themselves. They lose the joy of accomplishment which life would otherwise give them. They have failed to go far enough to search their mental "second-wind."

In everything worth attaining through human effort, there is a critical point where fatigue keeps us from going further. We may become discouraged. Discouragement is the off-spring of failure. But once that combination is broken through, we reach the higher levels for which we have struggled so valiantly. And stranger still, we become stronger, and more refreshed as we gain greater heights. Finally, each succeeding level produces in us a burning desire to push on to still higher levels.

Hence, it's very important to understand how to properly operate your greatest gift—your subconscious mind.

The Power of Suggestion

The subconscious mind is activated through suggestion. Our thoughts or willpower are the driving power, and current that connects our minds with the Divine, and Its controlling forces. Everything in our lives is triggered by our thoughts. In fact, the thoughts we hold express our desires or ideals. Thus, when we learn how to direct our habit of thinking, we will cultivate cheerfulness.

Affirmations are the primary force to activate the power of mind, and empowers us to attract the things and conditions in life we need for happiness.

You will learn more about the power of affirmations later in this work.

Money of the Mind Realm

Ideas are the money of the mind realm. Make of your mind the abiding place of rich thought. Do not wait until the million dollars appears before you to feel, and think like a millionaire. You are the child of the Divine who is the source of wealth. All that He has is yours—when you know It and think It and believe in It and live the richly royal life of a child of the Divine should live.

Like attracts like. A rich consciousness attracts the supply that will give it expression.

Whatever material wealth you may possess, your real wealth is in rich ideas. Material wealth has been known to vanish, sometimes with overwhelming suddenness. He who possesses only that form of wealth is in a precarious condition; for if the possessions are lost, he may not be able to replace them. However, if he is rich in consciousness and has cultivated a rich flow of ideas, he can call forth more wealth to replace his seeming loss. Moreover, if his mind is rich, the form of material that it attracts is likely to be enduring.

Neither ideas nor material wealth can be hoarded successfully. Refusal to give expression to rich ideas, with which Spirit blesses us clogs the channel. These ideas remain in mind awaiting expression, and more aren't likely to come until we have made way for them by passing on those which preceded. Withholding from expression rich ideas that come to the mind, is as much a form of poverty as is the withholding of material wealth from circulation.

For us to be truly rich, three things are necessary. First, we must become thoroughly conscious of the truth that rich ideas are the source of wealth. Secondly, we must cultivate the habit of rich thinking. To be mentally rich we must be constantly alert and receptive to new ideas, not only from the world about us but from the realm of the universal. The day of revelation is not ended, and we hear Him when we become still enough to listen.

A great mind means a great kingdom; one with untold riches—and power. It may be made still richer, more valuable, by the proper attention to its direction, and development of its natural resources.

All the real wealth of the world, all its art, music and literature, lies within the mind of man. Of what value is the fabulous wealth of mines, vineyards and orchards; of what use is the beauty of the universe, without the mentality to observe, comprehend and assimilate it all?

What we do with these ideas should be our gift to our Creator. We should seek to make our mind, our body, and our service to others the pure, capable channels for expressing His ideas. In doing this, we need have little concern about prosperity. When we conform to the law of prosperity, its expression is automatic.

From the universe about us we must gather the substance, the riches, we would store in our minds. Our consciousness, the practical, thinking, knowing part of us, constitutes the laboratory in which we bring about that metamorphosis which transmutes impressions into facts, and realities of our mental world. The value of those transmuted elements depends upon what we have chosen as the basis of our operations. And the kingdom of the mind is rich, or impoverished, according to the selections we have made, or the use we make of what we have acquired.

If we but stop to think about it, we can see that all we are dwells within us—each thought, impulse, inhibition, impression or ambition, must necessarily be measured by what we have within the range of our minds. Our entire wealth lies in that *Kingdom Within*, of the existence of which there can be no doubt.

How we can capitalize on the possession of this inner kingdom? I shall try to make clear.

Most people function near the surface level of their minds. They don't penetrate the store of unused energy which they naturally possess because exploration appears as a tortuous maze of concrete-laden tunnels, under massive mental mountain-like blockages. Before one can access the buried treasure, they must negotiate deep into subterranean and challenge imminent danger from deep water, falling rock, and the growing mountain underground labyrinths.

Thus only a small part of the mind is ever used.

Dig Deeper

Take the plunge into the deep and discover what lies beneath the surface of the consciousness: inheritance, wealth, resources, bounty, provided for your every need. All these are yours to draw upon at the command of "I Will!" They comprise a Divine inheritance, in truth; for the more insistently you draw upon the reserve, the more abundantly will it give forth, very much like a secret gold mine hidden in the hills, where you may go at will to dig out precious nuggets only to learn, as you return again and again, there still remains a never-decreasing store of riches.

How futile it would seem, however, to own a mine of great worth only to let it lie hidden. The zealous seeker for gold must labor, must toil and sweat, must apply the law of USE before he can lay hold on hidden wealth. This Law of Use is predominant throughout the vast universe. In every respect is designed for your good, for your happiness, your well-being—for your many-sided growth. The Law of Use complements the Law of Will. The instant you Will to succeed, you put into action the Law of Use. From that moment forward, it will be your privilege to tap the riches that a Divine Giver—the Source of all supply from the very beginning—meant should be yours: yours to use over and over every day you live.

What attribute, what faculty, and what material reward do you hold of greatest worth? You can Will it to become *yours* if you use your inherent powers toward that definite end. Do you want the lower or the higher, the poorer or the best? You can will yourself weakness or strength, doubt or faith, despair or hope, discord or poise, disease or health. You can Will yourself failure or success.

Which shall it be for you? The choice depends on your positive or negative thought. Your decision rests on whether or not you speak with power, the command: I Will!"

Will-to-Win is not nearly as important as the will to prepare to win.
Bobby Knight

8

Will Your Way to Success

If you hear a voice within you say 'you cannot paint,'
then by all means paint and that voice will be silenced.
Vincent van Gogh

It is not the mountain that we conquer, but ourselves.
Sir Edmund Hillary

Perhaps you have always thought of yourself as just "an average sort of person." You've never expected to go very far. You've settled down to being entirely satisfied with your lot. The urge to get ahead, the desire to become bigger and better, the call of your triumphant self, "to dare and to do," are higher aspirations that either never moved you, or they died out in you a long while back.

If you are not as young as you would wish, perhaps you sigh and say to yourself: "It's too late to begin thinking all over again now."

Why not change all this?

It is never too late to begin all over. Inertia, hopelessness, indifference, despair, acknowledged failure—these abide only in the grave. You—the *real* you, are not dead yet. Arise, turn-about-face; substitute for all this negative thought, the vitalizing and positive thought that's always at your command. Resolve to say: "I WILL." Henceforth, your spoken word will arouse positive thought; uplifting thought, thought powerful enough to generate a complete transformation in your whole life—yes; in body, mind and soul.

No doubt you have admired in others the fruits of success. Something deep down within you stirred a desire to become a success yourself. You pictured as in a dream the successful personality you, too, might be. Your momentary dream is but the pattern of the success you may eventually attain. Yet, fast upon desire must come the Will to succeed.

What Will You Do?

Tell me what *you Will to Do* and I'll tell you what you *are to be*. To heed this axiom—to adopt it as your very own—will release the power and the possibility of taking you wherever your heart may wish to go.

Your, "Will to Do!"

Think deeply upon it; apply it to your personal ambition; convert it into action; then prove to yourself, once and for all, how every latent aspiration will respond and take form to meet your insistent command: "I Will!" Thus upon the solitary *you* is laid either the penalty or the reward—the humiliation of defeat or the triumph of victory.

Yes! For everywhere throughout the course of life, in everyone truly awakened to the worth of human destiny, the training of the individual Will takes place on a testing ground where the weak strive along with the strong. In this domain, conflict is the price of praiseworthy existence. Here, "to the victor belongs the spoils," whether they are of material or of spiritual value.

Always in the realm of the hidden self, the conflict of the human Will—your Will and mine—against mediocrity or evil, goes steadily on. There is no obstacle too great to overcome by determined Will. Even the wall of stone is undermined, and eaten away by a constant pressure of water force against it.

Center attention upon that which is timeless, beginningless and endless. Strive for that conscious alignment with the Self which shall direct your days most profitably; which shall present to your vision *Truth*, and not its perversion or inversion; which shall enable your ears to hear that which shall strengthen and inform your heart and brain until they become true and conscious servants of the One: that Source which in truth is the Real Self of All.

With steady Will, there is no peak so steep that can't be surmounted. There is no way so hard it can't be trodden if determination be sufficient. There is no objective too great to be attained if perseverance shall endure.

Is this a mystery?

Recent investigations along metaphysical, as well as psychological lines, have demonstrated conclusively that thought exercises extraordinary power in our lives. Before we proceed further we must remember that after the subconscious has begun to do a certain thing it will continue to do that thing until the conscious mind directs or wills otherwise.

The subconscious can be trained to do anything; therefore, there is no limit to the possibilities that are latent in the being of Will.

However, we have tried to master mind and thought by simply using Will-Force, paying no attention to the laws through which the Will must act in order to demonstrate and exercise mastership.

A most detrimental group of half-truths has come from the belief that we can change our thought by simply willing to change our minds; also that we can change our thought without changing our thinking.

You change your thought, not by willing to change your mind, but by changing your mind about all things. You use your Will, not by forcing the mind to change, but in elevating the mind to a higher point of view.

Look at all things from a higher point of view, and all your thoughts will change without you trying to produce the change. Then if you give these changed thoughts action in practical application, and direct the subconscious to act with these new ideas and thoughts, you cause your entire personality to change.

Onward, if one wills wisely and well to a triumphant goal. Onward to the building of a higher, better, nobler self. Onward to a successful realization of the divine powers at the command of every living soul.

The change will invariably be a decided improvement for your entire life.

Money is the seed of money.
Jean-Jacques Rousseau

9

Plant Coins to Raise Dollars

Birds are caught with seed, men with money.
Armenian Proverb

Sow a thought and reap an action.
Sow an action, reap a habit.
Sow a habit, reap a character.
Sow a character, reap a destiny.

If you plant in fertile soil a hundred different types of seeds, you can produce clothing to wear, food to eat, homes for shelter, fuel to burn, oil to lubricate, turpentine, paints, resins, fruits, berries, vegetables: a thousand and one different products. These thousand different products come from the same soil, same sun, air, water and minerals.

What created the amazing variety?

What astounding intelligence told each of these seeds to draw the specific nourishment it needed to create such widely divergent products? Not man's mind, surely. Rather, it's the Infinite Intelligence of Divine Mind which answered man's call, or demand, the moment it was made. And, the weakest man alive has the Infinite Power like a seed folded within his being, and there it will remain until it's discovered and developed.

Ask yourself if the Infinite Intelligence is less kind to human life. Forces in humans are the same as the forces which underlie every part of the Universe. Forces are thoughts, and each thought is a seed of your own essence.

In the tiny seed is the energy, urge or desire to create the plant in accordance with the picture within it. In this way only, can the intelligence, mind or life in the seed express itself. In other words, the plant is the exact out-pictured expression of the picture or idea in the seed. The plant itself is not the life or mind in the seed, but the visible expression of that life or mind. In the same way, through a tiny cell or seed, man comes into visible existence. This tiny cell contains the life, intelligence, energy or mind necessary to produce the body of man. It also, contains the mental picture of the body the seed must create before that particular mentality can be expressed.

One thing essential to realize is that all seeds appropriates just what it needs from the boundless Source of all. The Source gives out according to the measure with which it has drawn. The plant draws from the soil, air and water just the elements it needs, transmuting these by an inner power called "life" into color, fragrance, and fruit. In an analogous way, man may draw to himself material for a higher life. The secret of this power is first to have faith that you have the power within you, then cultivate it.

There is one consideration: you must plant your mental seeds in that productive patch of earth which is your life, and those seeds must be planted in positive profusion, if you wish a healthy, happy, rich crop. A good seed sown in good soil *will* grow. If they are planted as seeds of negation, fear, worry, hate, intolerance, poverty and sickness; the same creative power will create them, but they will manifest as negative creations that destroy you. This same Divine Intelligence has the power to produce an oak tree, or a poisonous toadstool. It does not discriminate. You are given the intelligence to choose that which you wish to plant and reap.

"As ye sow, so shall ye reap" now becomes a scientific truth.

Deeds are Seeds

There is no room in the garden of the soul for the flowers of truth and falsehood to grow side by side. The latter will interfere with the growth of the former unless it's removed, while truth can only flourish when the soil in which it's planted is not depleted by the drafts made upon it by noisome weeds of falsehood. The choice between right and wrong must be made by ourselves, and we hold that all lovers of truth should welcome any and all revelations that will warn them of danger or make them conscious of the absolute reliability of the positions they have taken.

And can you not see that if you sow FREELY of wealth-filled thoughts, pure thoughts, healthful thoughts, you shall also reap abundantly of that which you have sown? But if, on the other hand, you constantly and continually sow corrupt seeds, how then can you expect to gather a harvest of perfect fruit or receive that which you did not earn?

Thoughts are Seeds

By now you understand that there is inside of you a Seed of Life capable of drawing to you any element you need, to bring to fruition whatever of good you desire. Do you want wealth, which is your natural state of being? Then turn your mind in the direction of wealth, THINK wealth, SEE wealth and wholeness, expect it, prepare for it and ACCEPT IT NOW!

Hold to the truth that there is a supply for every demand; then make intelligent mental demands for what you want. But do not expect things to come to you, if you do nothing else except demand, and sit still.

Demand of it that it bring you the elements you need for riches and success. Then take action!

The possibility of increase and multiply contained in one SEED (or ONE thought) is amazing, unbelievable and astounding, quite beyond the comprehension of the average person and, if given but a small amount of consideration, we become sobered and humbled before the Almighty Truth.

COMMAND—and KNOW THAT YOU RECEIVE!

Words are Seeds

The Word of Power is the prayer of faith, and the Word spoken in perfect faith by virtue of that faith manifests such measure of Reality into it that it becomes invincible to the desire for which it was spoken. It's not the power of the Word that brings back the fruit sought, but it's the Word of Power. The power of the Word may be a very limited power indeed, but the Word of Power is the Spirit of man speaking through his human organism.

The true secret, then, of material success in this world is to speak the Word of Power, but here again the untrained miscalculates, and finds his prayers not answered because he prays amiss.

It's the Word of Power that commands fate, but it can't be spoken too swiftly. There is another influence, another Law, than that of the individual Will, which determines the Word of Power. Words without power may be shallowly spoken, but the Word of Power having of its real content a faith born of the influx of the Divine Life into the human, falls into harmony with and under the law of Divine benevolence. And the Word of Power comes to be only that Word that stands in the correct relation in Truth. To be able to speak the Word of Power one must find his own center, and his own position in the universal relation, and then let the power speak out of his heart.

All the numerous insects and birds and beasts enjoy their lives in the provision made for them. Then feel how abundant the provision made for you, and learn to take of it in the right way and be able to say, "I am rich, I am strong and happy; life to me is full of joy and gladness; how glorious is it all!" And these words are seeds in your soul's garden.

Bless Your Seeds

It's the Seed of Divinity, the Seed of Life in YOU which your vision, your faith and your need have started into action. It's stronger than any circumstances. It can overcome any condition. So bless It. Stir It up!

Bless It morning and evening, but when the urgent need arises, DEMAND! Demand that It bestir itself. Demand that It draw to you whatever elements you need. Demand and give all as you demand all—make it a matter of life or death, survive or perish.

It's this which makes so successful the prayers of those who, demanding riches pour their scanty human store into the plate, and depend solely upon the Seed of Divine in them to supply their needs. When you can do this BELIEVING, the world is yours!

The Law is exact and accurate and everyone receives just reward, the entire amount of which has been earned. Furthermore, since there is a Divine Law of Sowing and Reaping, of Increase and Multiply, whatever seed, thought, word, action or effort you "plant" in the Invisible Substance not only grows until it reaches its maturity, but it also "bears fruit" or increases and multiplies. Successful life is a process of multiplication, adding to, increasing, and not of decreasing or subtracting.

Go wake the seeds of Good asleep throughout the world.
Browning

Moreover, this Law affects all life, from the least to the greatest and no thing having seed contained within it (in which is held the LIFE germ) can escape the Divine Law of increase and multiply, or of reproducing after its own kind.

When applied to the mental plane, to the realm of thought, this truth should cause us to become earnest, sincere and serious in our thinking. If we—all of us—could immerse our beings in the realization and understanding of the absolute truth of this inescapable Law, if we could but arrive at the needed point of determination to sow ONLY good useful seeds in the field of the mind, what a saving of reaping of tares, of whirlwinds, of sickness, or sorrows and disappointments there would be in this world!

If you, who read this, could inject into your mind and fully comprehend the meaning of the Master's statement, "Whatsoever a man sows THAT shall he also reap," you would at this moment, with all your might and main, with all the strength of your soul, determine to sow only such seeds (thoughts) as you desire to have increased, and speak only such seeds (words) as you wished to have "come true" in your life and affairs.

Nourish Your Seeds

Seeds are eggs, tiny eggs that require the correct balance of moisture, heat and warmth. In order to ensure success, It's necessary to protect your seeds. Money seeds are not much different in that they require the proper nourishment and conditions to thrive. Money seedlings are nourished at the beginning of growth with "soul" food. The embryo of your seeds must be fed with positive "soul" thought matter. Abundance, joy, peace, hope, contentment and happiness will produce a bountiful harvest.

The secret of a long and beautiful manifestation of money, here and now, lies in the soul. All physical and mental exercises are merely incidental and perfectly natural and not strained, with a spiritual being. The Spirit guides and assists Nature when we wholly rely on it and a spiritualized man or woman need give no thought to these incidental ways and means.

Do not allow your seeds to dry out with feelings of hopelessness before they can germinate, or they will die before given an opportunity to grow. Nourish your seeds with confidence, joy, integrity and appreciation. This protects them from being destroyed by the fierce flames and heat of anger, complaints, slandering or lying.

Do not plant your seeds so deep within your subconscious as to smother them before they can reach the surface. Provide nourishment for them daily in the form of affirmations.

Protect Your Seeds from Pests

One of the primary causes for lack of success is using thought seeds with shells that are *too thick*. Seeds of doubt or anger or other negative feelings are like pests (thick and hard); and like all other seeds the shell must be broken before the kernel inside can use its attractive power. And that shell is *thicker* and *harder* than the shell of any seed on earth. Thoughts of insecurity are like small delicate seeds that can't push up through "the dirt" of your thoughts. Only one thing will break it—and that is heat from within—a desire so strong, a determination so intense, that you cheerfully throw everything you have into the scale to win what you ever wanted. Not merely your work and your money and thought, but the willingness to stand or fall by the result—to succeed or fail.

Above all, be very sure, if you sow the seeds of wealth in the fertile field of your mind, that you permit no destroying "bug" to feed upon your growing plants, and thus prevent your receiving the harvest which you desire. Pests that prey upon the human mind, are as numerous and prolific as the innumerable hosts which feed upon the growing things of the earth.

There are as many kinds and varieties as there are minds to breed and contain them; but those most common to the ordinary individual are pests of worry, disbelief, fear, impatience, intolerance, envy, jealousy, rage and hatred.

The habit of grumbling, kicking, complaining and fault-finding is a pernicious habit which all who desire to appear well and be wealthy will avoid as they would a pestilence or a famine. Even a single one of these has the power to so increase, and multiply as to destroy you and your world. Take the world easy, and don't expend a bit of your vitality or energy in grumbling, or a bit of your precious time in looking on the seamy side of things.

And again, be careful to keep the lid (of your mind) tightly closed for there are some beetles which take a special delight in destroying the *green,* and growing shoots of prosperity.

Pull the Weeds. Plant the Seeds.

The attitude of intelligent demand, and hopeful expectancy, must inspire and accompany earnest effort if the desired results are obtained.

Cheerful, hopeful thought seeds have solved some of the great mysteries of life. However, do not expect sudden illumination. Do not imagine that you are to become perfectly well, perfectly cheerful and successful in a few hours or days.

Sudden illumination should not be expected in the process of Mind-over-Money. Mental power must be gained by degrees. This is an exact science. The Science of Correct Thinking. But the brain cells have been shaped by the old thoughts of hopelessness and fear. Thoughts like, "I am poor. I am weak and unhappy. Life to me is a failure," so says the faithless one. These words are like weeds in the garden of the soul.

These weeds can't be transformed all at once. Do not envision that you will become a millionaire, happy and victorious in a few hours or days. It's folly to think transformation of your whole being might take place in a week. Growth in Nature is unhurried. Some growth is rapid, other growth is normally slow. Mushrooms may spring up overnight, but trees grow with deliberation, and endure for centuries.

Look for gradual improvement, just as you might do if you were attempting to take up music or a science. The New Thought is a science, a science of Right thinking. But the brain cells which have been shaped by the old thoughts of hopelessness and fear can't all at once be reformed.

Remember: if at a quiet time you should find one such creeping, crawling thing lurking in the "upper room," of your mind, lose no time in exterminating it before it robs you of the peace and joy which is rightfully yours. And if you are not receiving the abundance which you desire, if prosperity seems to elude you, begin now to sow the seeds of abundance; but first make sure you have rooted up all those fast-growing weeds of belief in poverty and lack. Then FILL your mind with rich thoughts! Flood your consciousness with a prosperous feeling. You can imagine HOW you would feel if you *were* prosperous, can you not? Well, then, do that! Imagine you *are* prosperous. ACT THE PART and try to be a good actor at that. You may call this "visualizing" if you like, but the term doesn't matter much—it's the FEELING that counts, so put all the joy, the expectancy, the praise and thanks into your acting that you can arouse.

Germination – How to Make Your Money Grow

Germination is the process by which plants grow. All germination begins in darkness, in mystery and seclusion. How can you stir this boundless, mysterious force into action! How can you draw upon its infinite resource for your urgent needs?

Seeds vary in their requirement for heat and moisture. For instance, if they are over-watered and can't get air, they will perish.

Over-watering may be akin to sadness or despair or tears. Money seeds, like all seeds, can't survive when the environment is not balanced for germination. Money blossoms will bloom much longer and more abundantly; and the flowers will grow and produce more of its kind if they are treated with delicate care.

Faith

How much fortune you draw depends on the strength and depth of your faith. Utter faith—that is the only answer. No half-way measures will do. If you want help and have exhausted all the other methods, and you want now to go direct to the Source of new Life, Strength, new Health and Wealth, you can't keep dabbling with drugs and treatments, and hope to stir action. You must drop the Seed of Life in you into action. You must place your whole dependence upon the infinite power of that Seed of Divinity in you. You must get the attitude of our revolutionary patriots:

"Sink or swim, live or die, survive or perish."

You must be willing to demand of the Seed of Life in you to *bear fruit or perish*. Get that attitude of mind, and the stirring of your Seed of Life into action is simple!

Does that mean that you make no efforts to help yourself? By no means! This was never meant for a lazy man's world. The whole purpose of existence is growth, and all of Nature is continually growing. Whenever anything stops growing, it starts to perish.

You were given hands to work with, and consciousness to think with. You are expected to use them. You are entitled to just as much of the good things of life as millionaires, but it's not THEY who owe it to you. And it's not the world that owes you a living. The world, and they, owe you nothing but honest pay for the exact service you render them.

The one who owes you everything of good—riches, honor and happiness—is the Seed of Life inside you. Get to it! Stir it up! Don't rail against it. For you get out of it what you put into it—nothing more.

Don't go through life; grow through life.
Eric Butterworth

We are to use all our great gifts. And everyone has some; each individual makes some unique contributions to the whole pattern which no one else can. And the more we use these gifts, the more we have. Understanding increases by use. Love is not depleted by giving. The strength of muscles is not diminished by activity; rather, the reverse. Memory is made better by practice. It's better to wear out than to rust out, but why do either?

Suppose the sun said, "If I had not shone so much yesterday, I could shine better today!" The fact that it shone yesterday is the proof that it can shine today. Its function is to shine, and give light and it does.

Do you let your light shine, or do you hide it so that few know your good is working? The more our light shines, the greater our own illumination becomes. By sharing our good, we increase it.

Ready money is Aladdin's lamp.
Byron

10

The Art of Wish-Craft

Imagination is the wand of fairies.
Anonymous

Our hands contain a magic wand, this life is what we make it.
Adelaine Proctor

Aladdin rubbed the lamp. A burst of flame, the smell of sulphur! Then Genie appeared.

"Master," Genie spoke, "what is your wish?"

Aladdin gave his order and promptly the wish was fulfilled—jewels, palaces, authority, love; everything he wanted...

113

One hardly needs to re-tell the well-known story of *Aladdin and His Wonderful Lamp*. We recall how a poor truant child, came into possession of a magic lamp and an enchanted ring with which he could summon a powerful genie to grant his wishes. When he desired gold, silver, jewels, a palace and love of a princess all he had to do was rub the lamp to summon the genie and make his wishes known. And anything he wished for—fame, fortune, honors, happiness, love—he had but to command and the Servant of the Lamp produced it.

From a poverty-stricken youth, when he roamed the streets in search of odd jobs, Aladdin became, through the power of his genie, the richest man in the realm, second only to the Sultan in power and husband of the Sultan's beautiful daughter.

If you were told at birth that a strange and wonderful gift had been bestowed upon you, which like Aladdin's lamp, would bring you anything you desired in life, would you guard that gift fervently perhaps with your very life?

The desire to succeed, to achieve one's purpose and enjoy some of the good things of life, is an urge so universal and timeless that it's impossible to trace its beginnings.

History abounds with stories and myths of human desires, and secret powers hidden within.

In the world's masterpieces of art and literature we find many keys to the human heart; and this is especially true of the folk tales of the world.

Many of these tales are prosperity parables, in which hero or heroine is lifted out of the common run of experience, endowed with fabulous riches, and set in place of honor and authority. All too often such stories are dismissed as mere charming whimsy, but they are much more than that.

114

Actually, there is more than a childish fable to these old sagas.

It's said that folklore and fairy stories come close to Truth. Stories for children, and particularly those which have come down to us over a period of centuries, often contain hidden wisdom. Riches and honor comprise a favorite theme for these tales, and that theme occurs frequently. It's an idea dear to the heart of mankind, because it has its roots in all instinctive recognition of Truth.

The story-teller who gave us the tale of Aladdin was using the lamp as a symbol—a symbol of power we all can have. As Aladdin had only to rub his lamp in order to see beauty and riches everywhere, we have a lamp, too! However, Aladdin was granted merely three wishes.

We have boundless, infinite wishes through a power that is Cosmic and *meant* to be used.

But, where is this Cosmic Power. What is this magic? How do we activate it?

If you dig deeper into your true being, you will discover that manifesting is one of the ancient, secretive arts.

The power of thought, the magic of mind.
Lord Byron

A Realm of Riches is in Your Mind

The most daring of flights of imagination, the stories of miracles, authentic and otherwise, the varied creations of fancy's wide realm have never equaled the potencies and possibilities of the great Kingdom of Mind. The fact is, these tales and fables pale in substance when brought into comparison with the actual power of our own minds. All of the real wealth of the world, all its art, music and literature, lies within the mind. It contains a Realm of Magic, and these enchanted stories use symbolism to instruct us about the supremacy of our own souls.

Messages in all of these stories are similar. They teach us that our subconscious has extraordinary powers to attract invisible aides like genie in the lamp, magic beans or fairy godmothers, always ready to appear and help us to tap into our subconscious to realize our dreams.

From the Universe we can gather the substance, the riches of our dreams. Our consciousness, the practical and thinking and knowing part of us, constitutes the laboratory in which we bring about that metamorphosis which transmutes impressions into facts and realities of our mental world.

Directed properly with the Will, it has the power to create phenomenal wealth, health, and happiness beyond your imagination.

The value of those transmuted elements depends upon what we have chosen as the basis of our operations. And the Kingdom of Mind is rich or impoverished, according to the selections we have made, or the use of what we have acquired. A great mind means a great inner kingdom; one with untold riches—and immeasurable power. It may be made still richer, more valuable, by the proper attention to its direction and the development of its natural resources.

No matter how dark the outlook may seem to you, when you learn to use it correctly, there will be no inharmonious condition of circumstance in your experience which this light of true thought can't dispel, because the mind is similar to a magnet.

116

Magnetic Mind

What if someone offered to sell you a magic magnet that was guaranteed to draw to you whatever your heart most desired; whether riches, love or vibrant health? The chances are that you would buy it, or wish to buy it, no matter what the price.

The truth of the matter is you already have such a magnet. It's the powerful magnet of your mind. Already it's working in your affairs whether you realize it or not. But, in a great many instances, the magnet works against its owner, instead of for him, because he unconsciously uses it in the wrong way. The magnet itself is impersonal, and will draw things to us as we direct it. If unconsciously we use it improperly, we find, like Job, that "the thing that I feared has come upon me." On the other hand, when we consciously use it for our own good, we shall find that it's like a genuine Aladdin's lamp that brings us whatever good thing we demand of it.

That power is yours for if you take it. You have a right to it, and it's not necessary to work all your life for it, either. The big decision is ask yourself if you really want it. Making this decision sets the machinery in motion. Once in gear, you merely control the wheel.

Money is a magical phenomenon.
Osho

To many, money and magic is a strange combination. But money buys, and this is a form of magic like no other.

Our subconscious minds are as Master Magicians!

A Magical World

Thousands of years ago, the Wise grasped the fundamental fact—so hard for modern minds to realize—that deep within us, far under our outer layers of consciousness, is a Power that vastly transcends the capacities of any material hand or mind. In other words, each individual one of us has inner infinite powers, infinite capabilities striving to make us like our Creator! Think of it, a Force working in us can craft Magic for us.

Why, then, aren't we more powerful? Why are we limited by poverty, ground down by toil, wasted by disease?

Why?

We are like the fisherman who shut up a genie in a vase—we keep our genie corked up inside us, we tie his hands, we lull him to sleep and then leave him in the dark, while we try to do his work with our poor, weak hand and brains.

Instead of using our Divine right of dominion, we meekly accept conditions as we find them and reason step-by-step from them to their resultant circumstances, thus perpetuating limitation.

If we were mere beasts of burden like the horse and the ox and the ass, that is all that could be expected of us. If we were primitives, with no knowledge of our powers, you could understand such gutless submission to fate. But we are neither. We are sons and daughters of God, with all of His power latent in us—*and we know it!* We have only to waken the Kingdom of Heaven within us in order to get from life whatever we may wish.

Yet we plod along, looking to forces outside ourselves to raise our pay, or bring us more business or leave us a fortune.

Nothing external to you has any power over you!

118

We attract positive or negative conditions and events according to the nature of our thoughts. Frail thoughts are like weak magnets that have very little power to attract. Remember this when trials and troubles assail you.

God made you complete and self-contained. He put you in a world containing every element you need for your life and happiness. And He gave you, in your nerve centers (or subconscious mind), the means of drawing to you everything of good you may seem to lack.

You are, in effect, like a man sailing on an ocean full of fish. Deep down in the hold of his ship, under a lot of impediments, are nets that will bring him all the fish he can carry. But those nets are hard to get at and he has ready, to his hand, two good fishing lines that ought to be able to catch him enough fish to get along on.

So he uses them first. And if they don't bring him all the fish he needs, he rails against the ocean, or the fish, or the lines—but it never occurs to him to take a crack at himself for being too lazy to get out the nets that will surely bring in the fish.

Dreamland Lessons for Life

Recall, in essence all fables, fairy tales and nursery rhymes contain important lessons that reveal secrets for gaining fortune. The heroes and heroines all undergo incredible transformations. In order to receive things they desire, they have to do more than simply wish for them. They must take action to get them.

Through invaluable lessons, they learned the secrets to activate the power of magic. Jack had to climb the beanstalk to bring back the goose and the golden eggs. The wizard taught

Dorothy to click her ruby slippers. Aladdin had to rub the lamp! The godmother waved her magic wand.

From time to time we desire things, too, and fall short of obtaining them only because we do not put forth the necessary effort which, in some cases, is the equivalent to the characters' actions in these stories. Whatever you desire, whatever you dream, can be drawn through the power of your subconscious mind. But, as the fantasy characters, there are certain methods that you, too, must utilize in order to ignite the subconscious. It's as easy as uttering the command "Open Sesame!" and the genie we call our subconscious will rise forth to deliver wishes "at your command."

Desire is the rub of the lamp that sets Genie in action. Desire is akin to "Open Sesame" that unlocks the door to vast treasures.

"But," we object, "all our lives we've had the desire for wealth for a better profession, for authority. Desire doesn't help a bit! It sometimes seems that the harder we try the less progress we make!"

You tried *too* hard. You sidetracked the force of desire by moving down the blind alley of mere wishful thinking, which filled you with suspense and tension. *Trying* is admitting the possibility of failure. Instead of trying, just start succeeding. Don't worry if you miss your target with a rifle bullet. Cut loose with a machine gun.

Stop Trying—Start Doing

Trying, wishing, doubting, mere day-dreaming—all these cause suspense and tension. Tension is the resistance we set up within ourselves, and it's caused by fear. Horses pulling on a chain in opposite directions waste tremendous horsepower; they exhaust themselves but accomplish nothing. Pulling together, they are *force*. Power-of-Will versus Fear-of-Failure are the two competing horses that exhaust our energy, block our progress, and leave us with nervous tension.

"But," you claim, "Nervous tension is inevitable when we work! It's the way we are 'wired' up! It's natural to our temperament!"

Wrong!

Tension is that unnatural "monkey-wrench" in our machinery which should be lifted out. It's a short circuit in our wiring, causing our Fear-of-Failure to work against our Will.

Now, the warm knowledge that *our* Will is a part of Omnipotent Will "melts out" the short-circuiting monkey-wrench. We then stop acting like circling radio torpedoes that are out of control, and stop trying to set up in business for ourselves, by ourselves. We get back "on the beam" and hit our target.

Tension causes us to waste a hundred pounds lifting a ten-pound trifle. Tension is the brake which, when released frees our strength and enables us to become the mightiest warlord. Tension is fear. Freeing this tension, which wastes our strength, wrecks our plans and robs us of the power to make our hopes real, is as simple, basically, as was Aladdin's rub on the lamp. But in a complex existence, basic things are often overlooked.

Here is one way to go about it.

First, take a warm bath and go to bed. This soothes physical nervousness. Then realize that your Will comes from Omnipotence. Its natural flow does not stop while life continues, and it can't be shut off except when an unnatural dam of fear is put there by you. It's actually easier to release yourself and go forward than to hesitate. If you wish to make this contact with Omnipotence verbal, and call it a prayer, the result is even more positive. A broad feeling of courage and confidence is the immediate result.

Next, use the intelligence God gave you. You want something or you would not be attracted by the dream of Aladdin's lamp. What is it you want? What is the first step toward getting it?

If Only You Believe

You may or may not believe in the magic of mind, but unless you have tried its truths, exactly as you would try a chemical formula, and followed its directions exactly as you would a road map, and treated its "commandments" as conditions of its promises, you can't logically or sanely say that it's made up of wishful thinking, fairy stories or dream stuff.

To regard our legends and myths as purely fanciful creation, with no foundation in fact, is a mistaken idea. Very often they contain priceless gems of spiritual truths whose rare beauty are too ethereal to stand exposed to the material intellect. How fortunate we are in having those who, seeing past the dull drabness of ordinary existence, are able to find the mystic meaning and to picture for us, in story and poetry, in music and in art, what they have seen and heard on a plane higher than most of us have yet reached!

Hence, use your Magic Lamp of Truth, and stop cheating yourself! Stop cheating yourself by clearing your consciousness, your thinking and every destructive unwelcome fear thought. Have room for the joy that you would like to express.

This Principle, turning on the Light of Truth, or right thinking, as we call it, must be applied to every condition in your life. This you can do only by resolutely refusing to entertain, or think any negative thoughts about the conditions of your life.

In summary, the mind inherently contains hidden powers; electrical, magnetic, magical Forces. Mind is supreme. Our minds are the true builders of our world. A most magnificent gift is the subconscious mind. Like a magical genie, it waits for our instruction. However, when we misuse and misguide the subconscious, we bring endless suffering to our lives. Just as the most sacred stream of love can turn into a deadly tsunami of deadly hate, the erroneous use of the subconscious will bring about the most harmful effects in the your life.

Know that "where there is smoke there must be some fire." If great scholars, kings, emperors, scientists, generals and people who are successful in all walks of life, believe that Thought Power is the cause of their wonderful prosperity and triumph, what are you going to believe?

This is not mere theory. But you must prove it for yourself. So make a written list of all your unwelcome guests (harmful ideas) and for each negative thought substitute its opposite, namely a positive, perfect thought. Or, as I have so often said, hold in your consciousness, your thinking, the joyous anticipating of the thing you want to see come to pass. Then you will see for yourself that you are freer—happier—than you were before.

The art of Wish-Craft may be more complex than that of any other art form. Please try the experiment and prove the truth of what I say.

11

Magic Words Attract Money

Words are potent weapons for all causes good or bad.
Rudyard Kipling

Your Word is Your Wand.
Florence Scovel Shinn

You have used all manner of affirmations. How often have they accomplished "that whereunto they were sent?" Not often, have they? And you want to know why? Then read on.

Our Words Hold Mystic Powers

Robert Collier tells a tale of a shrewd magician who went to his king and told him he had discovered a way to make gold out of sand.

Since the monarch's kingdom bordered on a great desert, he had visions of fabulous wealth and offered the magician any price for his secret.

The magician named his price, then explained the process and departed. The process seemed quite easy, except for one thing. *Not once during the operation must the king think of the word "Abracadabra".* If he did, the charm was broken and the gold would not come.

The king thought that quite simply, especially as he had never heard of the word before, but, strange to relate, when he tried to follow the directions, he found he could not keep that obtrusive "Abracadabra" out of his mind. So he never made the gold.

Sounds silly, doesn't it, that anyone should be taken in by such brazen deception. And yet it's being done every day, with enlightened, educated people.

Worse, *we fool ourselves!*

For wherein are we better than the ostrich which hides in its head in the sand at the approach of danger, when we go through the motions of repeating affirmations of health or prosperity, while all the time our minds are full of "Abracadabric" words of fear that the charm may not work. Wherein are we better than the foolish king when we look to mere formulas for strength or riches?

Of course, they do not work! There's no power in words. It's only the IMAGE those words call forth that has potency.

"In the beginning was the Word," says St. John. What is a word? An idea, is it not? A mental image, an expressed desire. *"And the Word was with God, and the Word was God!"* When God took that idea to Himself as His mental image, when He put the life of His belief into it, it became part of Him, with all God's power to draw to itself the elements it needed to make it real.

That is the power latent in your words, when used properly.

Master of Manifesting

It's true that there is immense power in words.

King Features Syndicate columnist, Elsie Robinson, drives the point of personal word power in her syndicated column entitled *Listen World!* She tells in order to change your life and manifest happiness and prosperity, we must Keep Saying It!

The greatest medicine on earth... the most vital go-getter and potent force is – A WORD.

Do you want to BE something... DO something... CURE something? THEN PUT IT INTO WORDS AND KEEP SAYING IT!

There is an incredible force in words. They are not merely noisy air. They are the most important things in our lives. No charge of dynamite, no surgeon's knife, can alter life more deeply and drastically, for wealth or woe, than words.

And this isn't a rare occurrence. EVERY word is important. EVERY word does something to you, for you or against you. OUR LIVES ARE BUILT ON WORDS... MADE OR MARRED BY WORDS.

We spend years and fortunes in acquiring educations. We spend tremendous sums to "make a good impression." We fuss continually over grooming, charm and the proper mannerisms. But in the end we are judged, not by what we know or what we wear or how we act—BUT BY WHAT WE SAY.

WE EXPOSE OURSELVES WITH EVERY WORD WE UTTER. Even your slightest comment on the weather will reveal your character as surely as a police file and tell the world whether you're a fighter or coward, a POSITIVE or NEGATIVE character.

And words not only reveal you but they work for you. A word is an active force. It creates what you desire.

Secretly, insidiously, slowly but surely, the thing you say builds the thing you wish. You can talk yourself into heaven or whine yourself into hell---it's up to you.

Do you wish a rich and abundant life... life filled with challenge, change and opportunity?

Keep Saying It!

Affirm your desire. Affirm your faith in yourself. Affirm you willingness to take chances. Say it over and over and over. Say it to everyone who will listen. And, if there is not one who will listen, say it in an empty room.

KEEP SAYING IT... and the power in those words will go to work for you. It will enter into the minds of those who listen to you and shape their opinion. It will enter into your own mind—and mold your attitude. It will break down the prejudices of others and the fear that is in you.

And some day the thing you affirmed will come true. Then people will say it's a miracle. But it won't be a miracle. It will be a natural and inevitable consequence. You will have thought good fortune... talked good fortune... and believed good fortune... and GOOD FORTUNE WILL ANSWER YOUR CALL.

Do you want to be happy? KEEP SAYING IT! Do you want to be popular? KEEP SAYING IT. Do you want to be brave KEEP SAYING IT! Do you want to be well? KEEP SAYING IT!

Most people's creative minds are subconscious. You must learn to use it consciously. But unless you understand how the subconscious mind functions, you can't activate your creative minds.

Activate your subconscious mind by "Saying It!" Manifest your dreams by "Playing It!"

The Word Game

Are you master of your words? Perhaps you choose your words around the office, but what do you say in your home? Your friends enjoy your conversation, but how do your words re-act on your loved ones, when everything seems to go wrong? Play the word game for one week, and see how it can change your life.

I've tried this game many times with a class, and we always had marked results. Beginners in Truth need something definite to do. When we begin the study of music they give us definite exercises to follow daily. We show progress when we follow these guidelines.

Rules of the Game

This is the game: *I agree to guard my conversation against all negative words for seven days and to use only words that will promote Health, Happiness, Love and Prosperity.*

In addition to watching the words daily, repeat ten times aloud morning and evening Psalms 19, verse 14: "Let the words of my mouth and the meditations of my heart be acceptable in thy sight..."

Think of it, positive words of Health, Happiness, Love and Prosperity for seven days! Be generous with kindly words especially concerning the absent.

When someone gets out his little hammer and begins to knock, try to think of something nice to say about the person. There is truly some good in every human being. Recognizing the good often calls the better qualities of people into the open. We can always truthfully remark that perhaps we do not know how much some people are struggling against. This idea of speaking good words isn't generous, it's merely just to give credit for what they do or try to do.

Speak words of Health for seven days. "There is a light in your face today." "How radiant you seem this morning." Speak words of appreciation for simple things well done, words of blessing, words of gratitude, words of cheer and gladness, words of inspiration and strength. Too many people take the repetitions of favors for granted and quite as if such favors belonged to them by right.

Why not speak more words to show we are thankful. If we can help anyone to be happier, to be more successful, or more useful in the world we will be just that much richer ourselves. We only really possess what we use and share. In playing this game let us remember to speak words of love that we feel, but have grown to take for granted. Speak the words of faith in the future, courage and admiration for deeds well done.

One woman said she had never realized how negative her general conversation was. This word game changed the atmosphere of her entire home. She discovered that her words to her husband were usually blame or severe criticism, and she scolded and fumed at her children most of the time. This game saved her nervous energy so she was not so tired in the evening;

fits of temper passed away when the word game came in to play. Instead of saying "don't" continually she reasoned with her children explaining "Why."

Another woman always expected to awake with a dull pain in her head. Positive statements of the game made her radiant. The pain disappeared when she ceased to discuss it all day long and spent her thoughts on positive words.

A prominent club woman admitted that the members usually gossiped, but when she explained the game to them they all agreed to try it. She said it was really fun for they would stop any member who even started to voice a negative attitude. Since conversation can only be made about People, Things and Ideas, they tried discussing Ideas of a worth-while nature.

One man admitted he still talked depression to everyone who came to his office, but when he started playing the word game there was a general improvement in his business. A different spirit entered the atmosphere, and even his customers felt it.

After the class had played the game for a week each one had some outstanding demonstration of harmony in mind, body and affairs. Success will flood your life, too, if you will agree to constantly guard your conversation against *all* negative words and to use only words that promote Health, Happiness, Love and Prosperity. Affirm!

The Power of Affirmations

You must put yourself into the proper frame of mind by reminding yourself that Life is everywhere and in everything—in your home, in your business, in the very air you breathe. And that Life is able to draw to Itself every element It needs for Its expression. And, therefore, you already have in the invisible world of Mind, the means of bringing you anything you need by confident affirmation.

Feel free to develop and use your own affirmations. But if you have trouble starting, here are a few developed by Henry Harrison Brown in, *Dollars Want Me*, which have demonstrated proven results.

AFFIRM: I AM SUCCESS. THINGS BELONG TO ME. I AM ALREADY POSSESSOR. THEY WILL COME TO ME AT NEED. Then LET them come. If they are not, do not waste time trying for them. Having accepted Truth that ALL IS YOURS and that ALL DESIRED CONDITIONS or THINGS WILL MANIFEST, never think more of them. LET them come.

Until you hold your dreams as realities, they can't come. As Brown noted, you must change your attitude toward business. Do not seek it. SEE IT ALREADY YOURS and LET it come. He says, "Attend yourself to details as they come to the surface. Consider business a Principle that will run, as runs a mountain stream, when you remove your conscious Will from it. All your concern is to be ready to use it as the ranchman uses the water as it comes to his ditch."

Furthermore, he tells us Success "... is a manifestation of the One power. Use the Power as the telegrapher uses: LET it come and you direct it. The wisdom for the day comes with the day. LET it come by faith in Self. Work each moment as if it *were* here and it is here.

Brown says, "Regarding money, regard it also as merely the power that keeps business going. Welcome its coming and rejoice at its going. It never does its work until, like water in the stream, it has passed under the wheel.

"YOU alone are the Power. Money has only delegated Power. You direct its expression. Change your attitude toward money. It's not 'almighty dollar.' Almighty Power uses the dollar. Say to the dollar, 'I do not need you. You need me. You are of no use until my brain and hand use you. You wish to be used. You come to me that you may be used. Dollars need me.' Assume this mental attitude and see what a change it makes for you. When you have changed your aura, dollars will be drawn you need not worry about their coming. Only think of using them.

Dollars are but materialized thoughts. Each dollar in any hand represents thought in material form. Send out, at all times with your dollars, the thoughts you wish to return to you; for what you sow in your dollars, you reap in dollars that either do, or do not, come back to you. Put the thought of Success, Happiness and Health into every dollar that passes out and it will return so laden.

If you truly want to weave a tapestry of happiness, health, prosperity and success in your life, you must know the power of words. We all must understand that we make choices about how we think and what we say. This, in turn, affects how we live our lives.

> Talk Happiness!
> The world is sad enough without your woes.
> No path is wholly rough...
> Say you are well or all is well with you.

If opportunity doesn't knock, build a door.
Milton Berle

12

"I Am" is the Door

I Am love. I Am happiness. I Am healthy. I Am beautiful. I Am wealthy.

I Am grateful. I Am harmony. I Am that I Am.

Dr. Joseph Murphy, author of *The Miracles of Your Mind* and *The Power of Your Subconscious Mind*, explains the inner meaning of "I am that I am." He tells us that "I am the Universe and the Universe is me." When you say, "I am," you are announcing the living God within you. You are declaring yourself to be.

I am that I am. The first "I am" indicates what you want to be. And the second "I am" means the answered prayer, achievement and fulfillment of your desire or dreams or aspirations.

You feel yourself to be what you want to be. Do not repeat I am tired. I am poor. I am unhappy. Feel yourself to be what you long for; interested, fascinated, absorbed.

I AM is the Door to financial freedom, wealth and happiness. There is no other. There is but one Way. I AM is completion.

The Kingdom is finished. God is nothing less than whole. Man's access to the Kingdom of Riches and all it contains is through the use of I AM. Any statement made by man that is less than the completed Whole of I AM is a false accusation against Infinite Spirit.

It's because I AM is complete and limitless in its scope of action, that it brings forth so quickly. We never say, "I should be sick," "I wish I were poor," or "I want to be filled with disharmony." We say, "I AM sick," "I AM poor," "I AM unhappy." And through these statements, we meet the requirement of the Law; and we get instant and immediate results.

You have control over your world, because you have been given the use of I AM which opens all Doors for your entrance into whatever you desire. Your choice determines the use you make of his I AM. Approaching the Whole, you identify yourself with It by saying I AM. Ordinary conversation betrays the Son of Man, and crucifies the Christ. We more than crown Him with thorns when we constantly say, "I AM poor." "I AM sick," and "I AM a failure." Constructive use of the I AM, such as "I AM HEALTH," "I AM WEALTH," "I AM HARMONY," "I AM SUCCESS," glories the CHRIST.

We should not say, "I wish I were like Him." That is not enough. You are like Him, and your statement should be, "I AM DIVINE." One should not say, "I wish I had money." In Truth you are one with all Substance. "I AM WEALTH," "I AM ABUNDANCE," should be your thought. The statement "I wish" accomplishes little because it lacks definiteness and clear seeing. It does not identify man with the Whole, It is not complete. It will never open the Door.

"I AM THAT I AM, shall be my name forever" was God's promise to Moses. Jesus said, "Ask anything in my Name." What Name? The Name of the 'I AM THAT I AM."

"Hitherto have ye asked nothing in my name; ask, and ye shall receive that your joy may be full." Judging by the many unfilled desires and the restlessness of the masses, it's very evident that they have not asked, even though they believe that they are constantly asking and praying. They have not asked in "My Name," the Name of the "I AM."

How are we to ask in the Name of the "I AM?" There is only one Way, and that is the "I AM: Way—not the way of "wish," "hope," "maybe," "if," or "perhaps." We should not ask for health in a hoping attitude of mind; rather should we say, "I AM HEALTH."

That is true asking and praying. This is acknowledging the truth about ourselves; and is praying as though we received, which is the Jesus Christ formula for true praying. Did He not say, "What things soever ye desire when ye pray, believe that ye receive them, and ye shall have them."

This command of the Master requires perfect knowing—a realization of our oneness with the thing which we desire; and can we conceive of a statement which will enable us to feel that oneness more assuredly than the expression, I AM?

137

We are as children in the wilderness, wandering to and fro, with the Promised Land in sight—so near and yet so far. The reason for this is that we have not learned the way to possession, which is through the use of the Door—I AM.

The new mental actions will lead mind into new realms which will result in new discoveries.

How blessed will be this understanding to a thirsting world that is teeming with people who are hungering for the Truth. Precious children of God, they are yearning, seeking, and longing for a way out; and yet thy do not know that the Father of all is their abundant supply and that every desire of their hearts will be fulfilled when they realize their "I AM-AT-ONEMENT," and know that I AM is their Door.

The function of the imagination is, therefore, extremely important, but it's a function that few employ properly. Imagine feeling the wholesome, the constructive, the true, the greater and the ideal.

"Your heart knows things that your mind can't explain."

13

How You Feel Makes It Real

I don't want just words.
If that's all you have for me, you'd better go.
F. Scott Fitzgerald

What good are feelings anyway?
Nick Hornby

Much has been said on the question of thoughts and the degree to which they affect the general being of man. The very subject seems almost trite. We have become wearied of the mechanics of thought control and lost hope of ever gaining the results we seek through trying to so order our thoughts as to produce the results we deem desirable.

When we hear: "As a man thinketh within himself so is he," we often feel the helplessness of our situation. We haven't learned the secret of governing thoughts, therefore we are unable to control the outer conditions prevailing in body and affairs. But, whether we believe or don't, thoughts are rates of vibration which when sent out into the astral realm, acts through the magnetic mind to draw to itself whatever it deeply determines.

Resulting from search, the metaphysician has discovered that it's not mere thought which produces the various effects appearing in his being, but that the emotional state accompanying the thought is the vital causing factor. In this discovery we learned to place the emphasis upon the "within self," and styled it as a law beyond the mind and which includes the emotional actions and reactions.

Constructive thoughts *and* feelings are priceless magnets which call forth the hidden glory of happiness, health and prosperity.

So... you want money?

What are you thinking? How do you feel right now? You can't materialize money when you are thinking of lack. You must first change your state-of-mind. You must FEEL rich—you must RADIATE prosperity before prosperity will be drawn to you.

Stop thinking limitation. Think and feel abundance!

In order to manifest your dreams, your goal must be to feel good about them. Learn to tune out negative harassing thoughts—discouragement, bitterness, greed, pride, criticism, envy and lack. The whole power and effect of thought is in the emotional condition of the individual. This fact is easily revealed in the simple statement "I am happy." One can think "I am happy" and speak the words even forcibly, but unless the emotion which we call happiness is aroused, the thoughts and words themselves are of little effect. This is obvious to anyone who makes only a casual observation of his mental and emotional behaviors.

The law, then, seen in the foregoing light, would literally include "as a man thinks and *feels* within himself, so is he." In other words, that thought which penetrates into, and includes one's feeling nature, has become most effective.

The fact is that the emotional or feeling nature is the creative side of man's being, and whatever he feels deeply he is most likely to bring forth its corresponding manifest form. This would give evidence that one should guard his emotional nature with more persistent care than he does his conscious thought.

Start with Your Heart

As one studies himself carefully, he will discover that he actually lives more in his emotional nature or feeling state than his thinking state. Do not people talk more about their feelings than about their thoughts? Do you not describe your feelings, and concern yourself more about how you feel than how you think? It's true that our feeling nature does control and influence us more completely than our thoughts. But when understood this is only because previous thought has penetrated into our feeling nature, the creative machinery of our being, and has therefore developed and grown to greater proportions thereby.

However, in spite of the fact that man has given over the creative nature to a dominantly destructive state of mind, he still survives. Something greater than his own mind's thoughts, and his emotional feelings, has preserved him. He is, therefore, better than his thoughts and feelings would indicate, or that they have produced in his experiences.

Facing these facts we are forced to search for a still deeper meaning to this statement, "As a man thinketh within him, so is he." It must refer to something deeper "within him" than we have taught in psychology or metaphysics; it must refer to the innermost of himself, the very center or heart of his being.

In the next degree of revelation we find that it's more than a law of mind, or a law of the inner feeling nature. In fact, that it's not a law at all, but a mere statement of a spiritual fact. As a man is thinking in his most mysterious nature, is what reveals the true state of his being, is its real meaning.

From ancient philosophy we read this instruction: "Press the mind to lead all the senses into the heart. Thus shall the knower cross to the other side of the tempestuous waters of the river of illusion."

The ancient philosophers called all this field of thought moving in man's mind and feeling, the "river of illusion," and felt it was all false, not revealing the truth about the world or man, and that the true nature of man was revealed in the heart or innermost nature of all things. The "heart" does not mean an organ or any part of the body or mind, but the innermost fact. The center of anything is its Spiritual idea. Therefore, the heart or center of man, is the Spiritual ideal wherein is, and always has been contained, his real nature.

In essence, we are not the sum of all the thoughts that arise in our minds and feelings. We are the sum of the thoughts that arise in our hearts, from within, and the sum of these thoughts reveal the image and the likeness in which we were created from the beginning, and the fulfillment of these thoughts is the perfection of body and affairs which we now seem only to desire. It's the manifest result of the eternal command of our

Creator to "Be ye perfect, even as your Father in Heaven is perfect."

A power that lies dormant, and your ability to express it, is hidden from you until you are sufficiently developed and unfolded to be entrusted with its use.

You must train your feelings to reflect that you are what you wish to be. This is a time when new doors can be opened to larger concepts of life and some pattern can take shape and meaning—the old and the new fitting into place together. It is the manifest result of the eternal command of the God who created us to "Be ye perfect, even as your Father in Heaven is perfect."

French writer, and one of our earliest psychologists, Montaigne, learned a great deal about life by studying himself. He will say to you, "To live happily—to be a real success, that is—we must not only know ourselves, but become ourselves."

LANGUAGE

Clarence Edwin Flynn

The language of the mind is heard
Or read on a page:
The spoken or written word
Of lover or of sage.

The heart speaks not and writes no book.
It uses to express
Its thought a motion, song or look,
Or silent wordlessness.

The language of the mind is not
Long kept in mem'ry's store;
But what the heart says, unforgot,
Is treasured evermore.

The best way to have a good idea is have lots of ideas.
Linus Pauling

14

How to Get What You Want

If you're not actively involved in getting
what you want, you really don't want it.
Peter McWilliams

Yes! You've heard all of those formulas for success but common sense tells us we must be practical? Just saying, "Think success," and all that sort of stuff, means nothing. The law of attraction is not magic. It's not wishful thinking. It's an organized, systematic plan that will show you how to get what you want.

Motivational speaker and success author, Ben Sweetland, offers expert advice on how to develop yourself to get what you want through a parallel of how an engineer tackles a job to build a bridge. First, he says, once the engineer considers why the bridge is needed, for instance to span a certain river or canyon, he plans how it should be built. This might mean excavation, dredging, filling, etc. In other words, he would have to consider all of the resistances which might stand between him and the attainment of his objective.

Attraction Action

After he has taken these two steps (objective and resistances), what does he do? He draws the plans for the bridge based upon the conditions that exist—or, the resistances. To be successful, he must consider all resistances. If he should fail to include certain soil conditions or rock formations, he might later find that he would have a pretty picture of a bridge—on paper—but that it could not be built as designed.

Now we will build a success plan on these identical lines; and it will be just as infallible as the engineer's plan.

If you have been thinking while reading, you have discovered that there are three phases used by an engineer in any of his accomplishments: the objective; resistances standing between him and his objective; and his plan, based on those resistances.

Now, then to show how simple and practical this method is. Let us take a typical objective and follow through to see whether or not attainment of the objective lies within the realm of possibility. Before doing this, however, there are two important suggestions I wish to make. In connection with the objective, you should be specific. If, for illustration, you have always wanted to go into business for yourself, do not merely hold as your objective: "I want a business of my own." What kind of a business? Manufacturing? Wholesaling? Retailing? Where? City or country? Will you sell over the counter, through the mail, through jobbers, online? Etc., etc., etc.

After the objective has been clearly defined, Sweetland advises, you are ready for the resistance. And what I now tell you is very important. An engineer doesn't work with his resistances in mind and draw up his plans from memory, does he? Certainly not! He has every obstacle before him on paper, so that he can study them as he builds his plan. That is exactly what you are going to do. After you clarify your objective, you will take a paper and pencil and write down every resistance you can think of which now stands between you and the attainment of that objective. This makes your whole problem visual. You and see what you are doing. You are not stumbling around in the dark. Your plan of action will succeed because it takes into consideration your resistance; and they will be disposed of just as the engineer disposes of his obstacles or resistances. In fact, as you build your plan of action, in many instances you will be able to use your resistances as stepping stones toward success.

And now a word to you who might have been skeptical toward success formulas: Don't you agree that it's possible to plot out a course for success on a basis just as scientific as the rules and formulas used by engineers?

"Ah; but there is one circumstances where your method will not work," you say. And that in case you do not know what to do—when you have no objective.

The method can be used even if you have no objective. How? Merely the "finding an objective" as your objective and proceed accordingly. You then list those things (resistances) which have created the uncertainty in your mind and build your plan of action around them. It might be that you have no objective because you feel that, due to certain existing circumstances, you couldn't do what you would like to do. But the One-Two-Three Method will solve your problem for you.

Are you contemplating entering the field of salesmanship? Fine! Use this method. The sale becomes your objective. List all the resistances standing between you and the sale; then build your plan of action (sales presentation) to overcome the resistances. And watch your sales record grow.

Are you looking for romance, a husband or a wife? The plan works for such objectives, too. Focus on your desired soul mate. See him. See her. How do they look? How do they feel or smell. What kind of personality do they have? At heart, concentrate to raise your vibration. Write down your ideal relationship. And, write what you have to offer to the relationship. Be relaxed and open. Take action, go out meet people. You will be happy with the result.

> The distance between what you want
> and what you get is what you do.

Largely, what you are is determined by the character of your thought—not by chance thoughts, occasional affirmations or Sunday consciousness, but by your fixed habits of thought.

THE DAILY NEWS
NOVEMBER 1 - FASTEST DELIVERY
EXTRA! EXTRA!
MONEY
TALKS

When money talks, there are few interruptions.
Herbert V. Prochnow

15

Money Talks & Dollars Have Sense

When money realizes that it's in good hands,
it wants to stay and multiply in those hands.
Idowu Koyenikan

For the most, dollars are reasonable creatures. They are attracted to what they like and what likes them. If you are to draw dollars, you must learn money's language and follow money's advice. Let's start with the basics.

Basic Money Words: affluence, bacon, bank, big ones, bills, bread, bucks, Cs, cabbage, cash, clams, coins, currency, doubles, dough, ducats, e-Cash, five bits, fivers, fins, Gs, gravy, greenbacks, lettuce, loot, lucre, moola, pounds, riches, sawbacks, scratch, wads, wealth, pounds.

Called by many names, it's all the same. They all mean MONEY!

If you are to attract the big bucks to achieve financial freedom and success, listen to the following advice that money might give if Money Talks!

LB Rich: *Who do you most admire and why?*

Money: People with confidence. Someone who is willing to go the extra mile in order to achieve success.

LB Rich: *Why is right thinking vital?*

Money: This person commands a firm, steady, unwavering determination to win success and will do what is required to insure the realization of dreams. It's also important to be cheerful, optimistic and have self-confidence.

LB Rich: *How important is action in attracting money?*

Money: Think success. Talk success. Act as if you were successful. You must also rely on your own innate powers to succeed in all that you start.

LB Rich: *Please elaborate on the role of self-reliance.*

Money: Self-reliance frees one from being overly sensitive to what others say and think about him and his acts. Fear causes some people to be handicapped in following their ducat and dough dreams. They are afraid to be original, therefore, they miss much success that would otherwise come to them.

I would also advise them to be original. The world loves and respects originality and will pay for it in dollars and cents. Seek your own approval for your own conscience for all that you do, and then steer a straight course for the goal.

LB Rich: *What happens if they encounter disproportionate obstacles?*

Money: Obstacles should serve to call out one's innate power. If one plan fails, try another. Avoid getting into ruts.

LB Rich: *Why is it so much more difficult to demonstrate money than any other thing?*

Money: It really is not any more difficult to demonstrate money than any other thing once you have taken the proper attitude toward it. Mental tension, commonly called false beliefs or mortal mind, is the only thing that prevents anyone from seeing abundance.

LB Rich: *What are some of the success secrets for successful people?*

Money: Successful business people are always progressive minded; always by looking out for new ideas and new ways of doing things. Right thinking and right acting must go hand-in-hand if you are to achieve success. Follow your thinking by good solid work and use plenty of common sense.

LB Rich: *Can you summarize your uncommon secrets for getting more moola?*

Money: This may sound a bit unusual especially coming from money, but everyone should go outside to get sun to recharge. Like a magnet that needs solar recharging, your body, spirit and soul need to be recharged by the sun's energy. Once recharged, you can attract your desires like the magnet attracts metals.

LB Rich: *What can you say about the role of the mind?*

Money: Cultivate a cool poised habit of mind. Never allow yourself to form the habit of hurrying in either mental or physical work. Hurry and worry eventually lead to failure. It weakens nerve energy. It's important to live in harmony with Nature's laws and make the best use of your natural gifts. It's also important to develop concentration.

LB Rich: *Any particular advice regarding additional action readers should take to attract affluence?*

Money: Put yourself into every act of your life, however, trivial. This will help you to develop concentration and make work pleasurable. It's also very important to get proper relaxation and rest when not engaged in active work. When the business of the day is over, drop everything connected with it and relax mentally and physically. This will help to recreate the mind and body.

Few people really know the importance of keeping still and resting. To rest properly, every muscle must be relaxed, the hands and feet must be kept perfectly still and the mind made as near blank as possible. A little practice will enable you to banish disturbing thoughts from the mind during these periods of relaxation.

The habit of relaxation will not only keep the nervous system in good order, but it also gives steadiness and self-control to the mind. This will be found a great help to success because my money friends and I are attracted to the relaxed.

LB Rich: *Can you give some final secrets for attracting financial freedom... lots of money?*

If you truly want to demonstrate money, you have to gain the right idea about it. In order to gain a deeper understanding of how to create the state of mind to attract wealth, Money strongly recommends studying Rev. Ike's Ten *Commandments of Money.* These are proven principles that you can use immediately to transform your life. Here, he guides you along the path to wealth, health and happiness. You'll learn the proper way to think and talk about money; and how to develop the correct state of mind.

16

Core Secrets

I have ways of making money that you know nothing of.
John D. Rockefeller

What do you want with all your heart?

In any achievement of life—ability, fame, riches, love, spiritual power, moral perfection—whatever good and worthy aims you have cherished, whatever realizations you have prayed would someday come true—these can and will come true in exact proportion to the degree of will-power you bring to your everyday secret: affirmative thought, word and feeling.

Let's look within for your supply. Don't depend on your physical body only, not on your physical brain alone, but on your REAL self—that vast power of the Spirit which knows no limitation.

There is no situation that can't be conquered. Happiness, prosperity and abundance belong to all. The greatest bar is the lack of acceptance.

Throughout this book I have stressed repetition. It's important to study these lessons over and over. Apply them to your life until they become part of your life. You will soon experience the power of the unknown. You will manifest your wishes. You can now *bank on your dreams*.

Let us review.

Affirmations

The repetition of mantrams is hypnotic and people set their own limitations by leaning on the power of affirmations.

The moment we say, "I want a certain condition," we have barred the way to much good that we did not recognize, and have opened but one avenue of expression. Unless the statement were in accord with the fullness of an expanding life, the realization might take a form not anticipated. The very emphasis on *want* may aggravate the *need* instead of granting supply. The moment we put up a bar to the free flow of substance by a limiting statement, we hinder the perfect expression of Divine abundance.

What is the great expression that brings all things?

"I AM abundance."

This statement opens every avenue of expression and closes none. It recognizes the presence of God in all things and the conscious unity of the self with the source of all good. You will find this was the teaching of Jesus. It was abundance always with no limitation whatever.

"I AM knowledge." "I AM harmony."

Use of these expressions will vitalize the energy in the body so that there results a new awareness of the abundance of knowledge and harmony. The energy is not depleted through free use in daily life.

Our Creator Frees Us from Limitation

Worship of our Creator with all our hearts and all our strength frees us from conditions of limitation. No one need be isolated. It's possible to realize that sense of union with Divine abundance right now. The first determination must be an effort to get rid of the individual sense of limitation that we ourselves have built. There are several rather definite steps that must be taken to free the self from limitation.

Jesus taught in simple terms that the object of this life is a greater expression of life. Everyone is a unit in the whole principle operating in harmony, where every individual stands in his own domain completely in accord. For that reason you will find if you go through the simple teachings of Jesus that He put forth the declaration, "I AM God," for every individual to use. That is not a part of the Principle, but the Principle Itself.

Religious doctrines have all too often emphasized theory instead of practice. Repetition of such an attitude limits our understanding of Truth to the physical things and we lose the spiritual importance.

When Jesus was asked regarding the answering of prayer, he said that the reason prayer was not answered was that the asking had been amiss.

You will find that if you stand definitely with a positive declaration, you won't need to use words at all. The moment that you realize within yourself that abundance already exists for you, at that very instant the condition manifests for you.

Then you do not need outside suggestion. You are in perfect harmony with Principle. The instant you think of any condition, you are one with it. You will find that if you stand definitely with a situation, you will never need to repeat a petition. It's finished before you ask.

Jesus said, "While they are asking I have heard." Then He went right on and said, "Before it is spoken it is already accomplished."

Do we need to go on asking for a condition that is already accomplished? How many times can a condition be completed? Need we beg for something that is already ours? No! You can trace the lives of our greatest men and see how they accepted accomplishment. Deep in the subconscious the way of accomplishment already existed. With freedom from any sense of limitation they were able to express that which already existed.

It's through complete lack of division that we stand as Principle. How could we be in want if we put God in the place of want? Principle is harmonious and flows according to definite laws with which man must learn to work.

French psychologist and self-improvement specialist, Émile Coué, advises the routine repetition of the following affirmation: "Every day, in every way, I'm getting better and better"

Infinite power is at our disposal for any right purpose.

Secret Levels of Money

By now you know, Reverend Ike was one of greatest the Masters of Money Manifestation. He taught that in order to develop money consciousness, we must understand that money is a psychic entity. *This is the great secret!*

But how are you to individualize the infinite Power? How are you to bring It to bear upon your personal needs?

Rev. Ike offers the most important steps we need to take to develop money consciousness. He unveils the three levels of money.

Let's start at the bottom level.

LEVEL 3 – The **material level**. Most people are on that level and some never think of money any higher than the material level; the coin of the realm, the physical finance level and so. Though very important, this is really the lowest level. We need it on that level but most people stay there.

LEVEL 2 – The **psychic** or **psychological energy level** of money refers, more or less, to the level of comfort, material goods and wealth at the physical level. This is why we need to learn to think right and believe right about money because it really is a psychic energy. We should never insult or say negatives about money because as Reverend Ike, "Money has ears." And if money hears you talk or think negatively about it, it will leave you or never be attracted to you. You will repel it and always be in want.

LEVEL 1 – The **spiritual level** is highest level. It's where you come to the knowledge that you *are* that which you desire: You are "I AM." If you want health, claim it. Repeat "I AM Healthy." If you want to manifest money, repeat: "I AM Money." That is the highest level of money. From now on deal with money from that highest level, and it will emerge on the other two levels.

Exercises in Money Consciousness

You will find money materializing in various ways that intellectually you won't understand. This is not just an intellectual exercise, it's an exercise in consciousness. You have to exercise your consciousness of money and of all good on the highest level and realize that "I AM money." If you want to do healing, start from the spiritual level, "I AM healing, I AM whole, I AM well." And you will find that obtaining occurs on the physical level.

True love of the inner-self is always waiting for demonstration in your life. You must call it forth.

What, then is this powerful inner-self, this magnet of the mind? How is it controlled? How do we release these inner powers?

It has numerous names. Psychologists have glimpsed some of its possibilities and have termed it the "superconscious mind." Writers have sensed its presence; and we have the stories of the magic genie who obeyed his master's every command, and the myths and ancient legends of men who had access to a superhuman power. Some philosophers have recognized it and have called in the Supreme Reality and various other names.

Metaphysicians call it the Divine-in-You, the core of your being, or the Real You; the You that was created in the Celestial image. This Real You is one with Infinite Mind. It has the powers of omnipotence, omnipresence and omniscience. This inner being knows no limitations; it operates regardless of time and space. It has access to all knowledge. And, God-like, it's *creative* in nature. It's present in everyone; but most of us deny it by our beliefs in a limited world.

New Thought author, Stuart Braune gives us striking instructions for developing the magnetic mind that, if followed, will bring firm health, wealth, happiness results.

Know Natural Laws

In order for us to utilize the Powerful Magnet of the mind for our good, it's necessary for us to know something of the Law of Correspondence and the Law of Attraction.

Let us consider first the Law of Correspondence. In all the realms of life, physical, mental and spiritual, there are correspondences. "As above, so below" can be paraphrased, "As within, so without." Our so-called "outside world" is always but a reflection of our inner world or the mental conception we hold. "As a man thinketh in his heart, so is he;" and, also, as a man visualizes his world in his heart, so will his outside world be. This is the Law of Correspondence in action.

The kind of thoughts that go on inside a person's head are usually a replica of the things and circumstances in his environment. The Law works both ways. Those things that we "bind on earth" are "bound in the inner world." And those things that we "bind" within are "bound" without.

Walk into a person's office and take a look at his desk. Is it a jumble of papers, with nothing in its place? Is everything in his environment in confusion and disorder? If so, you can be sure that his thoughts are likewise confused and disordered.

Walk into a person's home. Is it slovenly? Is so, you can be sure that the resident of the house entertains slovenly thoughts, and the mental world is one of confusion. In such a home you are also more apt to find disharmony than harmony—more disease than ease. Harmony itself is order—disorder brings strife.

Thus we can see the "correspondence" between the physical plane and the mental plane. A disorderly, dirty, slovenly house, where nothing is ever in its place, is confusion

161

on the physical plane. Invariably you will find that people living in such conditions exhibit confusion in their mental lives. They are victims of inner conflicts, vague fears, bickering, strife, impatience, the inability to concentrate, etc.

Interestingly enough, this disorder and confusion in the mind also reflects itself in the body; and you are apt to find the occupants of the slovenly house suffering from various "disorders" of the body.

It sounds almost fantastic to imply that a good house-cleaning can be used as a therapeutic agent; but many people who have tried it have found it to be so. We are interested here primarily, however, with the Magnet of the Mind and how to bring it into operation in our affairs. This same Law of Correspondence can be of immense help in releasing these inner powers.

How to Use the Powerful Magnet of Mind

First, we must prepare the ground—we must utilize the most advantageous conditions for the manifestation of those powers. And one of the conditions is a calm and tranquil mind. Mental conflicts—even slight ones—inhibit the free and spontaneous action necessary for their manifestation. Inspiration comes in quiet moments, usually when body and mind are relaxed. If the conscious mind is occupied with thoughts of revenge, hatred, resentment, jealousy, etc., it's somewhat like putting up a red light to the inner mind. A person in the throes of resentment or hatred would be tempted to misuse and abuse these great powers of mind. Likewise, someone in the depths of depression would not have sufficient judgment to utilize them properly.

The first requisite, then, in using this Magnet "full strength" is to calm the mind. Great sages of all eras have advised periods of quiet meditation. Jesus, on many occasions, especially whenever he was facing a crisis, went away by himself. Yogis spend years in mental discipline, "taming" the "wild horses" of the senses. **They say that the mind must be tranquil and unruffled to contact the inner power.** They use a very good illustration in describing the importance of this "quieting." They compare the mind to a lake. When the mind has been calmed and the physical senses stilled—the passions and desires overcome—the mind become like placid lake.

On the other hand, physical desires and passions of all kinds are like waves upon this lake. The more violent the passions, the more ruffled the lake becomes. When this state of mental peace has been attained, conditions are favorable for the manifestation of the inner powers.

Now let us analyze the Law of Attraction. Briefly, it's simply this: "Like attracts like." In order to use the Magnet of the Mind, we must first of all attain the thing that we want within by visualizing it and "believing that we have it already." Bring as many of your physical senses into play as you can, because the law of Correspondence will see to it that the correspondences of our physical reactions will be reflected to our mind, and also that our concepts will be transformed into objective reality. See the thing you want clearly. Touch it. Get the feel of it. See it. Listen to it.

More Core Secrets

Another requisite for using this Magnet of the mind to attract the things we need, is that we must nurture within ourselves a BURNING DESIRE for the things we want. This desire injects the "breath of life" into the thought-image and activates it. It's not enough merely to "daydream" of the things we want. We must care enough about them to imbue our mental images with an overwhelming DESIRE. It's true that man can have anything his heart desires.

The apparent failures are due to the fact that the desire is not strong enough.

The third step in the program is to be willing to co-operate in the creative process by using our hands as well as our heads. When the farmer plants a seed, he can't make it spout. But he can, and should nourish, and tend the plant that springs forth— and he should not expect nature to gather his crop for him, and put in the silo. This is an example of the inevitable partnership between natural law and man. Each has a duty to fulfill.

This is the "natural" "scheme of things" by which the inner powers manifest themselves. Prayer was never intended to encourage a lazy man to "get by" without work. The old saying, "God helps them who help themselves," is truer than we know. It's somewhat analogous to the relationship of the brain and the hand in the human body. No hand in itself ever created a masterpiece of art, or did anything else worthwhile, until the idea and direction had first taken place in the brain. But, no man expects his brain to execute its ideas. Its job is merely to present them.

When invoking the inner powers bring us some particular thing, the "natural" course of events is to furnish us with some "inspiration" or idea, which often comes in a flash, or as a kind of "hunch." And nearly always these inspirations require our *doing* something. Then, we should "get busy" as soon as possible. Such inspirations needs not be "vague ideas." We have a legitimate right to seek guidance all along the line—even in the smallest details—as to what we should do.

It's All Within

Many of us, upon being told of this concept of the inner powers, are inclined to scoff: "Why, there's nothing in that—what's the use of speaking about some 'powerful magnet' if I've got to go out and do the work." This, however, is a superficial attitude.

Stop and think for a moment. Every single problem, regardless of its nature, could be solved by an *idea*.

"I don't know what to do is the common plaint of confused and miserable people. Now suppose you had a very wise man for a friend. And suppose that, whenever you have a problem, you could go to him, tell him what you need, and that he could immediately tell you what you must do to attain your desire. You would gladly "go through the motions" of the necessary work in order to carry out the plan that you *knew* could not fail.

Would not such a friend be a God-send?

This is precisely how the inner powers work—and there is power in the process, as you will discover. The magnet of the mind will arrange for you to meet a person that you need to know to further your plan. It will guide you to places where you should be. It will place in your hands the very book you need. Or a news item from the pages of a newspaper will leap out at you, giving you information that you need to round out what you are working on.

An amazing number of "coincidences" will occur that will give you just the "lucky break" you require.

Whenever these phenomena occur, always stop and acknowledge the inner powers at work. By thus recognizing the power at work, you will find that the "coincidences" occur more frequently. The very thing that you have been needing—the knowledge that you have lacked—will come to you by the most artful and astonishing routes.

This magnet of the Mind is yours NOW—waiting for you to use it. Remember these important steps—memorize them and try the plan for thirty days. Afterwards, you could not be induced to disregard it:

1. First calm your mind—clean out all resentment, fear, misgivings, ideas or emotions that would tend to cause mental turmoil. In order to achieve this mental serenity, see that your environment is calm, peaceful and in order. As Jesus said, "Enter into thy closet—and shut the door" against the outside world and all its petty annoyances.

2. Set the Law of Attraction into operation by forming a vivid mental image of the thing or condition you want. Make this image as "real" as possible by employing all the senses instead of merely the sense of sight.

3. Imbue your image or mental prototype with a *burning desire*.

4. Ask for guidance in what you should do to bring the demonstration into your affairs and be willing to do whatever is necessary.

5. When "things begin to happen"—when apparent "coincidences" or "lucky breaks" begin to appear, stop and acknowledge the inner powers. This last step is one of the most important of all—for it will strengthen and facilitate the use of the inner powers so that they will function daily

"In all thy ways, acknowledge Him and He shall direct thy paths."

Attention, Action, Faith & Visualization

There are four key words for you to remember to achieve success: Attention, Action, Faith and Visualization. By these you impress your subconscious mind with the desired picture.

Desire greatly. Desire earnestly and keep each desire simple, clear and single. Use your Will as a "blow-torch" in centering your attention on your desires.

If you are sincerely interested in something, you will have no trouble fixing your attention upon it. From the same root word, we get "tend" meaning to watch, and "tenure" meaning the act of holding, and "tenacity" meaning firmness (a bull-dog grip).

Since words are merely symbols of ideas, the subconscious mind accepts the full idea rather than the symbol. In fixing your attention on your mind picture, deliberately look at it at least twice a day, for ten or fifteen minutes, and as often as it presents itself to you. Do not strain to hold it long, but just let it go, and continue on your business. Remember the following:

- Smile until the smile sets for the day.
- Affirm you are going to be successful.
- Think optimism until you feel the exhilarating conviction that it's great to be alive.
- Visualize yourself having a successful day.

Because your mind is more receptive at night, impress your picture gently on the subconscious, just before you go to sleep. Cleanse your mind of all worry, criticism, hatred and resentment. Quiet your mind until it's like a serene, tranquil lake at evening. Like a star, reflected on the still water let your mental picture float in your mind. Or think of it as being impressed in soft wax.

In the morning, just as you awaken, hold your attention on your desire again. Assume a serene, but happy and joyous attitude and greet the day with a smile. There may be (and is) a great deal going on in the outside world, and very little of it's in the area of your control, but it's not selfish of you to be working on your own advancement. For when an individual attains his ideal of betterment for himself, he automatically lifts all those around him. It's like picking up a knot in a fish net. You raise all the other knots a little higher.

It's good, sound psychology.

The next two words are "visualization" and "action." They are closely related because your vision or picture should be an action picture, not a "still" picture. You should see yourself actually doing and being what you wish to do and be. If you want a pair of skis, see yourself using them, on the ski course with a merry group of ski enthusiasts. Make your picture a vivid dramatization of action!

If you desire a home, dramatize yourself living, working, cooking, eating and entertaining in that home. See yourself working in your flower-garden picking the flowers and arranging them in a vase. Use your imagination in seeing these things as if they were real, here and now. See yourself dressed in good clothes you want. It's perfectly right for you to be well-dressed, for good clothes give one the feeling of success and the attitude of success will bring success.

If you want a good job, find out what you can do well, what you really love to do, because your aptitude and efficiency will follow what you really want to do, then picture yourself doing that work.

You will find that as you impress your subconscious mind with your ideal, you will call forth new and rich ideas that will lead you to the right places, the right people, and the right circumstances to bring your ideal into reality. If you wish to improve your business, dramatize it as humming with activity, with orders, sales, production. Visualize other firms active and successful, as well as your own, for we are all so closely linked that, if we prosper, others will also.

Think Abundance! Be Abundance!

So, stop thinking limitation. *Think abundance!* *Be abundance!* Look upon yourself as a channel for Divine abundant supply to flow to all who come in contact with you.

There is really enough good and enough prosperity for all of us. Know that Life is working through you to express Itself in good to all. Think of yourself as a radio. God is broadcasting Life. And Life is power, understanding and supply. The particular service you have to offer is your means to making that supply manifest to your fellow man.

Why can't they get it for themselves?

For the same reason that music may be in the air all about you but requires a radio to make it audible to you. Well, Infinite Life is in the air all about *you*, and all about everyone, but it requires some means to make Itself manifest.

You are one of these means.

True, there are times when you seem to manifest only discord and lack. They are the "static" caused by worry and fear. But the music of life goes on just the same. So keep trying, and you will tune in and become a perfect channel for it.

The creative order, you know is from thought to condition. You can't materialize money when you are thinking of lack. You must first change your state of mind—you must FEEL rich—you must RADIATE prosperity before prosperity will be drawn to you.

So regardless of your present circumstances, let your thoughts be of abundance. Make your engine—your idea of giving service to your fellow-man. Then START IT RUNNING— no matter on how small a scale. After making your engine— your idea of giving service—put your Life energy into it—then release it by *setting it to work!* THINK abundance, and ACT AS A MEANS OF EXPRESSION FOR ABUNDANCE.

You know, the ancient Egyptians used to believe that to grasp an idea of anything gave you power over that thing, because the idea of it was to them the soul of it. The idea of money is pent-up energy. It represents just so much manifested effort, either physical or mental. But energy can expand only when it's released. *So start the expansion by releasing what you have!*

God has put into you seeds of Life in which there is more energy than is represented by all of Rockefeller's millions. All you need to do to accomplish is as much as he has, is to realize that you HAVE that Life-energy, that boundless WEALTH, and then proceed to RELEASE it by putting it to work!

Second—Create the spiritual picture—the nucleus which is to draw all riches to you. See your idea of service to our fellow man, as your means of expressing Life. Know that the Divine is working through you. That you are an instrument for individualizing the infinite Good, the boundless Life expressing through you.

Third—BELIEVE THAT YOU RECEIVE! SEE that Life in you DOING all those things you want It to do. SEE the abundant rewards of worth service pouring in. FEEL so sure of them that you can serenely GIVE OF WHAT YOU HAVE to start things moving, secure in the understanding that having Life, you HAVE every essential of success.

THEN, *Starting the flow*! No matter how little you have in hand, show your faith by GIVING of it to start things. Remember that the Law of Life is—Divide and Multiply!

So, bless the Life in you, and let It expand by releasing It and putting It to work And remember that God's Life has infinite power. It doesn't' matter how weak or unknown or poverty stricken YOU may be. It's not you that is doing the work—it's God's Life working *through* you. And whatever It undertakes, It can and will finish if you do not stop It with your doubts and fears. It's like a power line with unlimited electricity TRYING to get through to expand and work, but limited by the capacity of the tool to which it's connected.

YOU are the tool. You can choke it with doubts and fears until it will scarcely move a toy engine. Or you can run a transcontinental system with It.

Which are you doing?

"Don't look back, you're not going that way."

17

It's Up to You!

What happens next is up to you.
Chris Sacca

It's now up to you! Nothing can keep good from coming to you. By a scientific release of your spiritual energies can you become the master, instead of the slave, of your life.

You may not believe it when I say you are indeed a master-builder. But, your difficulties are your proof. They are a direct indication of your creative ability, for it takes just as much, or probably even more, ability to create negative, troublesome conditions as it takes to build the desirable things and conditions in life.

Of course, you say that you do not give directions for troubles and difficulties; you ask for the things that you really want. You pray for them and you think about them once in a while.

That is very good.

But of what do you think the rest of the time? Well, you very likely let your thoughts dwell on some of the disagreeable happenings of your life; you make your mind believe that your difficulties are real. You spend probably many hours of your day considering your failures from all angles.

If you seem to be sick, you "believe" that you are sick. You discuss your disease with anybody who is willing to listen, or you do the same with respect to your lack of money. You constantly reiterate the so-called "facts," and quite naturally your subconscious mind accepts those "facts" as the truth. It "believes." It has "faith" in your messages, and so it keeps on producing the situations in your life which are undesirable. Your disease and your troubles then stay with you. In fact, you build them more and more thoroughly into your life and your system.

If you have an unusual amount of trouble in your life, rejoice, for it is proof of your ability to use your mental and spiritual powers with effect.

Dismiss as false and unworthy of your real self, your higher and better self; all such negative, soul-destroying thoughts as "I am up against a blank wall"... "I am at the end of my rope"... "I'm a hopeless failure"... "Health, happiness and prosperity were never meant for poor, insignificant me."

THESE ARE THE VERY THOUGHTS THAT INVITE FEAR AND FAILURE.

174

There is a power, hidden deep within the consciousness of everyone, which enables them to rise triumphantly above every fear, worry and threatened disaster.

Always remember the great law of sowing and reaping: "Everything reproduces after its kind." To reap the fruits of positive demonstration, we must sow the seed of positive Thought.

No thought has inspired more people than the dynamic affirmation: "I am the master of my fate; I am the captain of my soul."

It's natural for us to desire to live in freedom from want and trouble and to manifest harmony and ease in our lives; yet it's apparent that this ideal state is enjoyed only by a limited number of people. Now you can too!

You can now fulfill your dreams and master your fate. You can have, do and be what you want. You can become financially comfortable, or you can develop your own business and earn millions of dollars. Do you want to live in a beautiful home and drive a luxury car? You can. Do you want to wear fine clothes, and eat at expensive restaurants? You will. Do you want to explore the world at stay in the finest hotels? You can explore the world. You can have servants. You can have instructors. You can be an instructor. You can learn new skills. You can teach new skills. You can speak new languages. You can have, do and be what you want. You can feel healthier and look younger. Enjoy happy, loving relationships. You can help people. You can help your community. It's up to you to be, do and have what you want.

Your mind is creative, and a creative mind will produce whatever you ask it to produce. The subconscious life forces of your mind do not judge; they are neutral. They take the thought material which you furnish them and help you transform it into manifestations in your outer world. They furnish the energy and the creative element.

You furnish the directions as to what should be produced.

The important thing is the realization that you are a creator; that those thoughts which predominate in your mind will tend toward materialization in your life. When you are fully aware of this fact, it's not difficult to change your mode of thinking from the negative to the positive side. When you really know what kind of thinking is the cause of your trouble, you will have no difficulty in changing over the opposite kind of thought. You will become enthusiastic over your power. You will learn to see the constructive, the positive side and the beauty that is inherent in every situation in your life. You will even see a ray of sunshine in your disease, and a silver lining on the cloud of your difficulties and hardships.

If you will then center your thoughts on that ray of sunshine, or on the silver lining, your subconscious mind will soon absorb the newly-discovered truth and will start to rebuild the foundation of your life. The state of discord will gradually make room for desirable things and conditions, and before long the same powers that created distress and failure for you will lift you up to the pinnacle of joy and success.

It's principally a matter of shifting the "gears" of your mind from reverse to forward, from negative to positive, from despair to hope.

Time flies, it's up to you to be the navigator.
Robert Green

The power that makes Man the "Master of his Fate" is a power that resides within.

"Mind," wrote James Allen, "is the master-weaver, both of the inner garment of character and the outer garment of circumstance."

Use your mind to alter your life. Concentrate upon every part of the brain several times every day. Concentrate upon your heart. Impress upon the idea of genius upon every cell. Always breathe deeply and steadily while concentrating in this manner, and draw to the brain all the extra energy generated in the system at the time. Through this simple process mental and emotional capacity and ability are remarkably increased.

Try it... NOW!

Remember, what you do is up to you!!

*****

I BARGAINED with Life for a penny,

> And Life would pay no more,
> However I begged at evening
>   When I counted my scanty store;
> For Life is a just employer,
>   He gives you what you ask,
> But once you have set the wages,
>   Why, you must bear the task.
> I worked for a menial's hire,
>   Only to learn, dismayed,
> That any wage I asked of Life,
>   Life would have paid.

Coming Soon

ADVANCED MONEY-MAKING SECRETS

Learn More At:

www.cashcut.money
info@whatIwant.club

CCC
Cash Cut Core
Box 543
Highland MD 20777